This Was John Calvin

Thea B. Van Halsema

BAKER BOOK HOUSE
Grand Rapids, Michigan 49506

*In memory of
my father, Clarence Bouma
through whom I met John Calvin*

The daughter of a seminary professor, Thea B. Van Halsema grew up in a home which was deeply committed to John Calvin's interpretation of the Bible and in contact with Reformed and Presbyterian churches throughout the world. Her interest in Calvin was later enhanced by travel and study with her husband, Dr. Dick L. Van Halsema, who is president of the Reformed Bible College in Grand Rapids, Michigan. The Van Halsemas have five grown children.

This Was John Calvin was written in 1959 for the 450th anniversary of Calvin's birth and has been translated into Spanish, Portuguese, and Indonesian.

Preface

This Was John Calvin has been written to tell the story of a life. It is an attempt to make the man John Calvin real, to recapture something of the amazing, inspiring person he was. It does not pretend to discuss his theology—this has been done often and well by others who are qualified to write of such things.

It is surprising to find how much we can know of Calvin's life from his letters and writings, from the records of his day, and from the many reliable books which have been written about him. I have benefited from these, and from days spent in Strasbourg and Geneva during the summer of 1958.

This book has been a joint enterprise in our home. My husband provided materials, suggestions, and inspiration for the writing. He also edited and indexed the manuscript. For all this, and more, I want to thank him.

I am also grateful to Dr. John Kromminga, President of Calvin Seminary and Professor of Church History, for his kindness in reading the manuscript.

When Calvin died, his friend William Farel said, "Oh, how happily he has run a noble race. Let us run like him, according to the measure of grace given us." I hope this telling of the Calvin story will give inspiration for the race each one of us must run.

T.V.H.

Grand Rapids, Michigan
April 3, 1959

Contents

Part I
"God So Led Me"

1

The woman and the boy came out of the dim cathedral into the sunlight of the corn-market square.

As usual, the square was crowded with people and animals. Millers who had sold their sacks of flour prodded their donkeys to return to the country. Men on horseback clattered over the cobblestones. In blacks and browns the priests and monks went on their way.

The woman saw little of this as she moved into the noisy crowd. Her eyes were still misty with the emotion of her confessions. Her lips had scarcely ceased their prayers to the saints. People called her a pious woman. She was as pious as she was beautiful, they said, and that meant she was pious indeed.

But the boy, half hidden in the fullness of his mother's cloak, looked out with his sharp little eyes and saw everything.

11

Threading their way across this hub of the town, the two came home. They went in softly because home was also an office. Behind the leaded, greenish-glass windows the head of the house sat at his table carrying on the business of the church. This Gerard Calvin was attorney for the priests and canons. He was secretary to the bishop himself. The men who worked for the church were always passing in and out of his door. They wrangled and shouted in his ears. They schemed and maneuvered to advance themselves. They got into trouble and needed their lawyer to get them out. Gerard Calvin worked tirelessly in his important job for the men of the church. He was a shrewd man, respected by everyone. He was also shrewd in watching out for his own interests.

The church attorney was pushing ahead in his little world. He had been pushing since the day he left his father's village and his father's trade. Why be a cooper, making casks and barrels, when one could wield a pen instead of a hammer? Half an hour from his father's home, in the French walled city of Noyon, the son of the cooper settled down. People said Gerard Calvin was fortunate when he married Jeanne le Franc, pretty daughter of a rich, retired innkeeper. Their first child was Charles. The next two infant sons died. Then came John, the boy with the sharp little eyes, seemingly a favorite of his parents. He was born at twenty-seven minutes after one in the afternoon of July 10, 1509. After John, there was born one more son, Antoine.

Perhaps it was the plague that killed beautiful Jeanne le Franc Calvin when her son John was only three years old. A stepmother came into the home of the three small boys and added two daughters to the family.

Years later, though he rarely mentioned his early life, John wrote about a little pilgrimage he had made with his own mother. Together they had walked two hours out into the valley to the shrine of Saint Anne, earthly grandmother of the Lord. Lifted by his pious mother, young John kissed the precious relic of the skull of Saint Anne as it lay in its golden receptacle, surrounded by candles and flowers and the adoring faces of other pilgrims.

This was said to be a very special relic, this piece of bone. Its shrine was always crowded. One could stay right in Noyon and find other relics, all faithfully worshiped as real. In those days people were ready to believe anything. There were supposedly some hairs of John the Baptist, a tooth of the Lord, a bit of Old Testament manna, and some crumbs from the New Testament feeding of the five thousand. In the cathedral was a fragment of the crown of thorns. There were also lesser relics like the remains of a certain Saint Eloi. The monks of the saint's abbey and the priests of the cathedral were always fighting about where these bones really were, in the abbey or in the cathedral. It was a furious, endless argument. Even the French parliament was not successful in solving the matter.

For fourteen years the boy John lived in Noyon in the French province of Picardy. Ten thousand people lived within the walls of the old city. It was then already old. Five hundred years after Christ Noyon had become the seat of a bishop. Here the great Charlemagne had been crowned king of the Franks in the year 768. In the twelve hundreds there had gone up, stone upon stone, the massive, dark cathedral which overshadowed everything else in the city.

13

Noyon was overloaded with priests, monks, canons, chaplains, and every other kind of church employee. Each was intent on his own rights and his own advancement. Over them all ruled the powerful bishop, a nobleman of the family de Hangest. The cathedral was the center of the city's life. Besides it, there were monasteries, churches, and chapels in abundance. Each had a bell. Each bell rang often. There was a saying in Noyon that one could not speak three words without being interrupted by a bell. The tolling of the bells floated over the valley. Especially on feast days, the pealing chorus reached the ears of bargemen taking their flat crafts down the River Oise toward the sea. The bells echoed almost to the row of low purple hills that caught the sunset in the evening.

In this small walled world of shrines and relics, of processions and feasts, of tapers, bells, and images, the middle son of the church attorney grew up. He took part in it all devoutly, remembering the misty eyes of his mother. But from his stool in the corner of the house he also heard the voices at the desk of his father. Perhaps it was a churchman arranging to get the fruit of more vineyards or the grain of more fields. These men were always grasping for things. They were always seeking to be richer, to be more admired.

Perhaps, in bed at night, John wondered with the thoughts of a boy. . . .

The Lord, whose lifesize image hung upon the cross in the cathedral, bleeding, wearing only a loin-cloth and a crown of thorns—on earth He was not rich in things. . . . And was He pleased with these men who worked for Him in the church? . . . Was He happy to see them grasping and cheating, wearing splendid robes, setting themselves up? . . . Was He?

2

Gerard Calvin looked out for the future of his sons. He needed money for their education. Since he then planned to train them for the church, he took advantage of a common custom and arranged to put his boys on the church payroll. In those days a boy could be appointed to a church office, collect the salary, pay an adult priest a fraction of it to do the work, and keep the profits for himself. One had to know the right people to work out such plans. It was against the law, but the law passed out of sight on this point. There had been a pope, Benoit IX, who was only twelve years old. And an archbishop of Rheims who was only five when he received his office. And a bishop of Metz who had just turned four. Charles de Hangest himself, bishop of Noyon, at the age of fifteen had received from the pope every kind of benefice and the revenues that went with them. People had stopped being surprised at this sinful bargaining for jobs in the church.

Gerard Calvin knew the right people in Noyon. He watched for openings for his sons. It was arranged that Charles, the oldest son, become chaplain of a little chapel when he was just old enough to sing in the cathedral choir. Three years later, in May of 1521, young John received his first benefice. He was appointed to one of the chapels of La Gesine, for which he received each year three measures of corn from one town and the wheat of twenty grainfields from another. Father Gerard paid a priest to do the work of the chaplaincies and kept the rest of the profits for his sons. It was a neat arrangement.

Twelve-year-old John solemnly signed the oaths of the chaplaincy. Next he received the tonsure, a special haircut that left the crown of the head shaved. The new little chaplain with his grainfields and his shaved head was now a priest-to-be. He had money for study.

A chaplain could exchange his benefice for a better-paying one if there was an opening. When he was eighteen and studying in Paris, John exchanged his first chaplaincy for another, passing the first one on to his younger brother Antoine. Again, two years later, he made another exchange and became in name and salary the chaplain of nearby Pont l'Evêque where his grandfather Calvin lived.

The de Hangest boys, nephews of the bishop, were good friends of John. These boys liked the church-lawyer's son even though he was not one of their aristocratic class. John played at their mansion. They taught him to ride a horse. He studied with them under a private tutor. Later he went with them to the Collège des Capettes, a small boys' school in Noyon named for the hooded capes its pupils wore.

When the school of the hooded capes had nothing further to offer, the de Hangest boys prepared to go to Paris to study. The plague had returned to terrify the people of Noyon, and this was another good reason for leaving the city. Would John like to go with them? they asked. John was enthusiastic. His father eagerly grasped the opportunity. The canons of the cathedral met and decided, a bit reluctantly, that John's income from his chaplaincy would not be cut off if he left Noyon.

It was summer 1523 when the de Hangest boys and the son of the church attorney, with their escorts, rode off on horseback from the plague-infested city where they were born. Eagerly they galloped toward the great city of Paris, sixty miles to the southwest. John Calvin, aged fourteen, was riding into a new world of people, places, and ideas. He would never again be back in Noyon to stay.

3

Things were happening in the world outside Noyon.

On the pope's throne in Rome sat Leo X, wearing the triple crown of his exalted office. Leo X was a de' Medici, the most magnificent of all popes, the man who supposedly said, "What a profitable affair this fable of Christ has been to us." Whether he said it or not, he made a great profit out of his office. His riches were unbelievable, his art treasures amazing.

Leo X was also busy building the grand Saint Peter's cathedral in Rome. But money was not coming in fast enough; so he devised a new money-making scheme. Anyone who pays something toward the building of Saint Peter's in Rome will receive an indulgence, a paper certificate, saying that his sins are forgiven. So declared the magnificent Leo. These indulgences were supposed to be good also for the sins of dead relatives waiting in purgatory. In 1513, when John Calvin had just turned four, the monk Tetzel began his tour of the German states, selling indulgences.

It was this monk Tetzel whose arrival stirred up another monk, a doctor of theology who was teaching in the University of Wittenberg. Martin Luther had begun to teach there a year before John Calvin was born. In 1517, when the boy of Noyon was eight, the professor of Wittenberg nailed his ninety-five theses to the door of the Castle Church. The forgiveness of sins cannot be bought with the money of indulgences, Luther proclaimed. Forgiveness is free, the gift of God, not of pope or church. The sound of the monk's hammer in Wittenberg signaled the beginning of a reformation for which many people were ready and waiting.

In the mountains of Switzerland, Ulrich Zwingli was ready. The monk Samson of Milan was selling indulgences to the Swiss people, but Zwingli preached so mightily against him that Samson could not get permission to enter the city of Zurich. Instead, Zurich invited Zwingli to become parish priest in its Grossmünster church. He began his new work with a series of sermons on the Word of God, preaching from the Scriptures which men had not heard for centuries.

Men had not seen the Scriptures, either. It was the more wonderful, then, when there appeared in Basel in 1516 a fresh Greek edition of the New Testament by the great Dutch scholar Erasmus. A lost book rediscovered—that was what it was.

In France, with its fifteen million people and its long coast lines for trade, things were also happening. Here the Reformation began with a distinguished old professor in the greatest university of Europe. Jacques Lefèvre was teaching at the Sorbonne in Paris. A native of the province of Picardy, a learned man, a traveler in Africa and Asia, he had come back to teach and write in Paris. Here at the age of seventy he rediscovered the truths of the Bible.

In the year 1512 when Luther, still unknown, was seeking peace for his soul, when Calvin was three years old and toddling with his mother on her pious rounds, Lefèvre published his Latin translation of, and commentary on, the epistles of Paul. It is God who saves "by grace alone," said the old professor.

Among the pupils of Lefèvre was a stocky, red-bearded fellow from a mountain village. The student was energetic, fearless, quick, and forceful in his speech. He was also searching. "My son," said the old professor to this student one day, "it is all grace." Almost suddenly William Farel saw with the eye of faith what his learned teacher was telling him. From that day on he was afire with zeal to preach everywhere the rediscovered truths of God's Word. "God will renovate the world," said the aged Lefèvre to young Farel, "and you will live to see it."

Others followed the old professor in bringing back the Bible. In the town of Meaux near Paris a bishop named Briçonnet opened The Book and found new answers there. He began to reform the congregations under him. He preached from The Book, a thing unheard of in churches of the pope. Briçonnet was an influential man, welcome in the palace circles. Here, too, he spoke. The king's sister Margaret was converted, and Briçonnet put the Bible into her hands.

Excitement ran high. Lefèvre was translating the New Testament into French so that the common people could read it for themselves. He worked at Meaux, with Briçonnet encouraging him. Farel came there, too, and busily went to work among the people. The wool carders and weavers of Meaux, the peasants and vinedressers of the districts around—all were reading and talking about the Bible. Their churches changed. Their lives changed. In those days it was often said of a man converted to the faith of the Scriptures, "He has drunk at the well of Meaux."

As the new faith spread in France, its enemies stood up to stamp it out. Chief among these were two men in high places. One was crafty Noël Beda, head of the Sorbonne University. The other was greedy Antoine Du Prat, the chancellor of France. At first these men and their helpers used threats and arguments. When these failed, they used fire and the hangman's noose.

In the middle of the struggle stood the French king, fickle Francis the First. Sometimes he listened to his sister Margaret, who devoutly embraced the new faith and was always pleading for its followers. More often he was pressured by the Beda-Du Prat group, who accused him of betraying the holy church and of allowing terrible heresies to arise in his kingdom. Francis I had more power than most kings of his day, who bowed to the wishes of the pope. France had not bowed. Her kings often bargained with the pope and sometimes forced him to their terms.

But the pressure was on. Lefèvre was put out of the Sorbonne. In 1525 his writings were condemned, his New Testament publicly burned. Still he continued to work at Meaux. Writings of Luther began to make their appearance in France, smuggled in and translated for the people. They were on the Sorbonne's black list of forbidden reading. So was a little book by Margaret, sister of the king. So were many other writings which the Sorbonne called heresy. Anyone found possessing such writings could expect to pay dearly. But the people read anyway. Printers printed in secret. The whole French capital was seething with the conflict.

Into such a Paris came John Calvin and his companions from Noyon in the summer of 1523. John found his way through the narrow, twisting streets to the home of his Uncle Richard Calvin, a blacksmith.

It was August, the month in which the smoke of a human sacrifice went up from the Place de Greve. A converted Augustinian monk was tied to the stake and burned for his "Lutheran heresies." He was the first to die that way in Paris, the first of many.

4

In the Collège de la Marche of Paris was a well-known teacher who asked to teach beginners instead of the advanced students to whom he had been assigned. "I would rather give the new boys a good foundation in Latin and French," said Mathurin Cordier, a former priest, known all over France for his excellent teaching.

John Calvin was one of the fortunate boys before whom Cordier laid open the world of good grammar. He taught his students Latin and good French. When the mature Calvin later wrote in fluent Latin and in vivid French, he had Cordier to thank for a foundation in these languages.

Twenty-seven years later Calvin did thank his good teacher by dedicating to him the commentary on First Thessalonians. "It is fitting that you should come in for a share of my labors," writes Calvin in the dedication. "When my father sent me, still only a boy, to Paris . . . , Providence so ordered it that for a short time I had the privilege of having you as my teacher, so that I might be taught by you the true method of learning."

The boy of fourteen also made an impression on his forty-six-year-old teacher. Cordier was so attracted to his pupil that many years later he came as an old man to Geneva to teach in the academy founded there by Calvin.

On the left bank of the Seine River, among the colleges of Paris, there was one that was known to be the oldest, the gloomiest, and the dirtiest. This was the Collège de Montaigu, a school for the study of theology. To it Calvin was transferred after he had spent three pleasant years studying the arts in the Collège de la Marche.

The Collège de Montaigu was famous, but not for good reasons. It was famous for lice and bad food, for the stinging lash of whips that punished the poor or the slow student. No boy might speak a word of French at any time. Only Latin was heard in the dark, damp corridors. Calvin stayed in the friendly home of his Uncle Richard, but the poor students who boarded in the college were up at four to start lessons. John, too, had to get up long before dawn to ride his horse to the gloomy place.

"Oh, how many rotten eggs did I eat there!" said the scholar Erasmus about his year in the Collège de Montaigu. The great French writer Rabelais had an apt phrase for the lice that swarmed on the walls, in the beds, and on the black-robed boys. "The short-winged hawks of Montaigu," he called them.

The director of this college was a man named Tempete. The students nicknamed him in Latin "the terrible tempest." Before him there had been the flinty Noël Beda, heresy-hunter and head of the Sorbonne. Beda still came there to teach the art of nimble Latin debate. How is a hog led to the market, by the rope tied to its neck or by the farmer who pulls the rope? On such and more serious topics the boys learned to argue for hours.

Calvin drove himself to master all his studies—the Latin classics, the logic, and the writings of church fathers like Augustine and Thomas Aquinas. He was eighteen years old when he finished the course and received the master's degree. His stomach often bothered him. His head often ached miserably. But his young mind had triumphed over all of this. It was keen and disciplined and ready for use.

Fortunately, during these grueling years Calvin had friends. Sometimes he saw his friends from home, the de Hangest boys, nephews of the bishop. His cousin Robert from Noyon was also in Paris. Robert had been converted to the new faith, and he later became known to the world as Olivétan, translator of the Bible into French, Protestant missionary to the villages of the French Alps. No one knows how often the cousins talked and argued together about the Church of Rome and the truths of the Bible as Lefèvre and Luther and others were rediscovering them.

Calvin made new friends in Paris, too. It was amazing that a teen-age boy, alone in a big city, could become so well liked by people of importance. The king had a Swiss physician named Cop, a man of learning. Calvin was a close friend of his four sons, especially Nicolas. Many times he visited in the Cop home, listening to fascinating conversations about new ideas. He was also in the home of Guillaume Budé, the most brilliant new thinker of France. Budé's son was Calvin's friend. There were other friends, also unusual people. Apparently they considered the young man from Noyon to be unusual, too.

5

Some startling events occurred in Paris in the five years that Calvin was there at school. In 1525 Francis I lost an important battle with Emperor Charles V of the Holy Roman Empire and was locked up in Madrid. Angry and humiliated, he was there for a year until he arranged to have his two young sons kept as prisoners in his place. It was a surprising defeat for France. Louise of Savoy, the mother of the king, ruled while Francis was gone. She had no patience with heresies. The Sorbonne could count on her.

Lefèvre, the old professor, fled to the German city of Strasbourg on the west bank of the Rhine. Farel, who had been busy in Paris, escaped to Basel. But Briçonnet, the bishop of Meaux, wavered. He had led his people to the truth, but he lacked the courage to follow that truth to prison, exile, or fire. Instead he bowed to Beda and the Sorbonne, acknowledged his "error," and ordered the Protestant preachers in his bishopric to be silent. And so he kept his bishop's mitre, the beautiful headpiece that was a sign of his place among the eighty-three honored bishops of France.

But the common folk of Meaux put their bishop to shame. They were not afraid of the fire. There was the man Denis who, before going to the stake, rebuked his bishop. And the youth Pavane, who spoke so movingly to the crowds as he stood at the foot of his faggot pile that one Sorbonne doctor said, "I wish Pavane had not spoken, even if it had cost the church a million in gold." There was the so-called Hermit of Livry, for whose burning the bells of Notre Dame cathedral tolled to call the people to witness. And the wool carder Leclerc, who in his misguided enthusiasm had broken in pieces a statue of Mary. For this offense he was pulled to pieces with red-hot pincers before the flames killed him. Could the student Calvin have been in Paris during these times and not have gone with the crowds to watch one of the fiery executions?

Meanwhile, in Rome, the pope himself was in trouble. Clement VII, who came after the magnificent Leo, was locked up for seven months in a tower in his own holy city of seven hills. He, too, had lost a battle with Emperor Charles V. In 1527 the troops of the emperor scaled the walls of Rome and took it. They looted the city. Soldiers made sport riding through the streets in the red robes and hats of cardinals. Church documents were ripped up to make straw for the horses. Art treasures were slashed. Some uncouth fellows even got down into the tomb of the warlike Pope Julius II and took the ring from his dead hand.

While Clement VII was holed up in his tower, helpless until he made terms with the emperor, a delegation of men from England arrived in the looted city. Their king, Henry VIII, the king of many wives, was then ready to get rid of his first one. Would the pope grant him a divorce from Queen Catherine? Clement VII was in trouble enough. He had no wish to make Emperor Charles angrier by giving a divorce to the king of England. No, he said, he could not grant it. Henry VIII found another way. He created a new archbishop of Canterbury, who declared the marriage invalid. The next year Henry VIII made himself head of the church in England. He was done with the pope. England was on its way to becoming a Protestant country. God had used a woman and a divorce to change the religion of an empire.

Not only kings and popes were in trouble. In Noyon Gerard Calvin had his troubles, too. For some reason he had refused to produce certain records of accounts. The churchmen were provoked with their attorney. Perhaps Gerard Calvin was also provoked with them and disgusted with their greed and conceit. With this brewing in his mind, father Calvin gave more thought to the career of his son John and made a new decision. He wished his son to become a lawyer.

"When I was yet a very small boy," wrote Calvin years later, "my father destined me for the study of theology. But afterwards, when he considered that the law commonly raised those who followed it to wealth, this prospect suddenly induced him to change his purpose. Thus it came to pass that I was withdrawn from the study of philosophy and set to the study of law."

Martin Luther, when pressed by his father to study law, had forsaken it to go into a monastery. Calvin, interestingly, never questioned his father's order that he change his career. Obediently he set out for the city of Orléans, whose university was famous for its faculty of law.

In 1528, about the same time that Calvin left Paris, a shabbily dressed Spaniard entered its gates. Ignatius Loyola, thirty-seven years old, had come to Paris to study. He brought with him a donkey loaded with books, a purse holding a few gold pieces, and the written set of rules for a Society of Jesus. The virgin Mary herself, said Loyola, had dictated these rules to him in a cave near Barcelona. The Spaniard who entered Paris would one day be honored in the Church of Rome as the founder of its strict, powerful Jesuit Order, which began as Loyola's Society of Jesus.

The young Frenchman leaving Paris, his master-piece as yet unwritten, would be even better known as a brilliant champion in the Protestant camp, a defender of the truth rediscovered in the Word of God.

6

Orléans was a wonderful place. The students of its university lived without a care. They played the game of "rackets" on forty tennis courts. They sailed in little skiffs on the river. They had endless banquets and parties. The fame of the law professor l'Étoile and his colleagues had attracted students from many countries.

But the student from Noyon did not take part in the feasts and revelries. More than in Paris, if that were possible, he drove himself deep into study. For supper he usually ate little or nothing, so that his mind would be clear in the evening. He allowed himself only a few hours of sleep and then lay awake an hour in the morning, reviewing all he had studied the night before, developing his memory, filling it with knowledge. Within a year Calvin was known more as a teacher of law than as a student. Sometimes he lectured as substitute for professors who were absent.

Calvin studied more than law. In Orléans there was a man named Wolmar, a German with Lutheran leanings, a fine teacher of Greek. Calvin applied for lessons. From Wolmar he learned the language of the New Testament so that he could study its books in the original tongue. He devoured other Greek writings as well. Perhaps while Wolmar taught his pupil Greek, he also pointed out the meaning of certain New Testament passages which were dear to Luther and the reformers.

To this Greek tutor Calvin later dedicated a commentary, the one on Second Corinthians. "Under your direction," wrote Calvin gratefully, "I added to the study of law Greek literature, of which you were then a celebrated professor."

After a year in Orléans, Calvin went to Bourges, a city destroyed by Caesar, rebuilt by Charlemagne, and now lying in the province under the rule of the king's sister, Margaret of Navarre. She had invited the renowned law professor Alciati to come from Italy to lecture in her university. Wolmar, the Greek professor, also had been invited, and found it safer, no doubt, to be a Lutheran under Margaret's protection. Many students wanted to hear Alciati. Calvin joined the group that came to Bourges. In Wolmar's house he met a young lad whom Wolmar was tutoring. Calvin then was about twenty years old. Little did he dream that the twelve-year-old boy, Theodore Beza, would someday stand with him and be his successor in a city neither of them had yet seen.

In 1531 Calvin was back in Paris for a short time. There the news reached him that his father was seriously ill in Noyon.

And so the son of the church attorney went back to the house on the corn-market square. It was strangely quiet behind the greenish-glass windows. The men of the church did not stop to inquire about the sickness of their lawyer. Their quarrel with him was not settled. In addition to this, brother Charles, who had become a priest in the area, was also in trouble with the clergy. With these clouds hanging over him, Gerard Calvin died in May of 1531. His sons, say some, had to plead with the canons of the cathedral to allow their father's body to be buried in holy ground instead of in an unmarked hole in some empty field.

Twenty-two-year-old John stayed a month in Noyon after his father's death. He and Charles turned in the accounts which their father had refused to give the clergy. John conducted a service in the little chapel of Pont l'Evêque, where he was in name and salary the chaplain. During the days at home he listened to his brother's bitter complaints against the church and the clergy. Perhaps the brothers chuckled together about the Noyon bishop and his beard. The bishop had refused to wear his beard short, though there was a rule about this in a church law book. He had arrived at the cathedral in his splendid robes one Sunday, wearing the mitre and carrying the golden cross. But the canons shut the big doors in his face and told him to take his long beard and go home. So he went.

These days also provided time for brotherly talk about other things—about the ideas of the old professor Lefèvre and the pamphlets of Luther, about flinty Beda and his companions in the Sorbonne, about fickle Francis and his pious sister, about the smoke of human sacrifices in Paris and in Meaux.

The month at home brought time for thinking, too. The church attorney of Noyon was dead. His middle son John, who had respected his father's wishes without question, was now free to make decisions for himself. Not to the church, with its greed and rigid thinking, nor to law, a specialty of the sciences, did Calvin turn. The life of a scholar enchanted him. To learn more Greek and Latin, to use these languages and to read the literature written in them, to search the old writings, to write about them, to retreat into a book-filled study—what more could one ask, except a little money with which to rent a quiet room, buy a scanty meal of food and wine, and lay up enough ink and paper with which to write one's ideas?

And where else but to Paris would one go to live such a life? King Francis had recently made Paris more attractive to the scholar. Under the urging of Budé, the king set up a new College of Royal Lecturers, much to the irritation of the Sorbonne. This was part of Francis' interest in the new thinking and learning, known as humanism, which was sweeping Europe.

Everywhere people were beginning to think for themselves, instead of letting the church do all their thinking for them. Those who were able read the wisdom of earlier centuries in Latin and Greek, using this wisdom as a basis for their own thinking. This new humanism was not Christian, but it had one great value. It encouraged people to do their own thinking rather than to accept blindly what the church told them. People who now began to study the Scriptures for themselves were discovering much that the church of those ages had hidden or ignored. In the lives of many, God was using this new learning to help them back to His truth.

Having decided to be a scholar, Calvin set out

from Noyon for Paris, walking the sixty miles. When he arrived, a friend offered him lodging, but he chose instead to rent a room in the dormitory of the Collège Fortet. It was closer to the colleges where he would attend lectures. The lodging was up a winding staircase, in a row of narrow, cell-like rooms, where students and teachers alike lived and studied.

Eagerly Calvin plunged into his study of Greek, Latin, and Hebrew. By day he made his rounds of the lectures. By night a candle burned late in his study cell. He was learning, studying, writing. Calvin moved again in a circle of unusual friends, scholars like himself. He was back in the house of Cop, the king's physician. He was taking part in the learned talk of the Budé home. This was the life he wanted, wasn't it?

While Calvin bent over his books in Paris, Ulrich Zwingli, the reformer of Zurich, died on the battlefield. He had gone out as chaplain with the Protestant troops of his city to repel an attack by other Swiss troops who were fighting for the Church of Rome. As Zwingli knelt to comfort a wounded man, he himself was wounded and later killed by the thrust of a spear. Revengefully, the enemy quartered his body and burned it. It was October 11, 1531.

But the student in Paris, if he heard the news of the battle of Kappel, did not pay it special attention. He was deep in his books, writing one of his own, besides. He could not know that one day he would adopt Zwingli's country and become known as a reformer even greater than the forty-eight-year-old man who had just been killed under a pear tree in a meadow near the high road.

7

The book was written. It had taken seven or eight months of hard work, not including all the hours spent on lectures and studying. With a young scholar's pride, Calvin took his handwritten manuscript to the printer whose shop was at the sign of the Two Cocks. He had sold some of his meager belongings to pay part of the printing cost. The rest of the money he had borrowed.

The book was dedicated to his childhood friend, Claude de Hangest, nephew of the Noyon bishop. Claude was now abbot or head of Saint Eloi's monastery in Noyon. "Accept this, the first of my fruits," wrote Calvin. "It belongs of right to you, for I owe to you both myself and whatever I have, and especially, because I was brought up as a child in your house."

In April of 1532 Calvin's book came from the printer. It was about an essay of the Roman philosopher Seneca, who lived at the time of the apostle Paul. This was the popular thing for scholars to do—to read famous old writings and then to write about them. For a first book from an author only twenty-two years old, Calvin's *Commentary* on Seneca was an astonishing piece of work. It was written in excellent Latin. Calvin had quoted with authority from fifty-six Latin writers, twenty-two Greek writers, and seven church fathers, besides writers of his own day. There were only three insignificant references to Bible passages.

But the book did not sell. It went quite unnoticed. Calvin begged his friends to buy the book, to recommend it to others, to ask their professors to use it. He sent a copy to the scholar Erasmus in Basel. Still the book went unsold. While it was bad enough to be ignored as a new author, it was worse to be in debt personally for the printing of the book.

Still, this free-lance life of study and writing was what he wanted, wasn't it? It was. And yet—perhaps it would be good to finish the course of law that was interrupted by his father's death. The little trunks of books and other belongings were sent on their way to Orléans. Calvin followed after them, walking.

The fame of the thin, brilliant student who never went to parties had lingered in Orleans from Calvin's previous year of study there. Respectfully, the students who came from the province of Picardy elected Calvin to manage their affairs. They grumbled when, instead of throwing a big party to celebrate his election, he gave the money he would have spent on the party to the university library for the purchase of books. But they respected him none the less.

Again Calvin stayed in Orléans about a year. The next summer he left it in a hurry, called to Noyon by his brother Charles' increasing trouble with the church. John's course in law was almost finished, but apparently he did not wait for his doctor's degree. Back at home on the corn-market square, he watched the demonstrations against heretics and so-called Lutherans. He attended a meeting of the clergy, of whom he was officially still a part. What he did to help his brother Charles is not known.

It was September of 1533 when Calvin went back to Paris and took lodging with a cloth merchant, Etienne de la Forge, who lived in the House of the Pelican.

Three months later Calvin was fleeing for his life.

8

The people of Paris were excited.

Nicolas Cop, the young rector of the University of Paris, had made his annual All Saints' Day address to the university. Instead of talking about the saints and the holy church, Cop had used the text, "Blessed are the poor in spirit," and had gone on to talk about the gospels and God's free grace. He had spoken against the persecution of those who were turning back to the Bible. He had quoted Erasmus, whose works were banned by the Sorbonne, and some of his words sounded strongly like Luther, though he did not say whose words they were.

The professors of the Sorbonne were furious. Two monks rushed over to parliament and demanded that the rector be prosecuted. They could not rush to the king because fickle Francis was down in Marseilles, arranging to marry his second son to a niece of the pope, who had come by ship to meet the king.

There was another strange thing about the rector's address. It was whispered that in writing it he had used the advice or the help of a young scholar named John Calvin. After all, Nicolas Cop had been a friend of Calvin for ten years or more. They were often together. What would happen to them now, with the power of the Sorbonne attacking them?

Late in November 1533, almost a month after his address, Nicolas Cop started out in academic procession for the palace. In his rector's robes, with the beadles who carried his golden staves of office marching before him, he was on his way to answer a summons from the parliament. Suddenly a messenger met him, carrying a warning from a friendly parliament member. Flee for your life, said the messenger. The Sorbonne has persuaded the parliament not to release you. The king is out of Paris and cannot save you.

Nicolas Cop turned into an alley, shed his cap and robe, disappeared into a crowd of helpful students, and was out of the Saint Martin Gate in disguise within an hour. He left so fast that he took the university seal with him.

This escape was too much for the chief police lieutenant. He sent his bailiffs to get John Calvin at any cost. But the students had outmaneuvered the authorities again. While some made talk with the bailiffs at the foot of the stairs, others helped Calvin escape through a back window down a rope of bedclothes. In the home of a friend who owned a vineyard, Calvin put on the working clothes of a vinedresser. He left the city with a hoe over his shoulder, walking north toward Noyon. The bailiffs had his books and papers, but they did not have him.

What had happened to Calvin to make him a hunted man? Until then he had been known, if he was known, as a brilliant student, a young author, a rising scholar, a man still promised to the priesthood. These new ideas that he shared with Nicolas Cop, that so angered the men of the Sorbonne—when had they taken over his heart?

Calvin had heard these ideas for many years—from Lefèvre, Luther, Zwingli, whose writings he had read. He had heard them from his cousin Olivétan, who had argued many hours with him when they were students together. He had heard them from his Greek teacher Wolmar, for whom he had deep regard. He had even heard some of these ideas, spoken in bitterness, from his brother Charles, now excommunicated from the church for his heresies. Calvin had found these ideas for himself when he learned the Greek and Hebrew with which to read the Bible in its original languages. More recently he had seen these ideas in action, in the fires of the martyrs, in the home of his pious landlord de la Forge, whose house was a secret stopping place for believers from everywhere.

For a long time the heart of John Calvin had not been ready for this truth. "The summit of my wishes," he said, "was the enjoyment of literary ease, with something of a free and honorable station."

"But . . . though I had some periods of quiet, I was still far from true peace of conscience. . . . And the more closely I examined myself, the sharper the stings with which my conscience was pricked, so that the only solace left to me was to delude myself by trying to forget it all. . . . I was pursuing the course which I had begun, when a very different form of doctrine started up, not one which led us away from the Christian profession, but one which brought it back to its source and, as it were, clearing away the dregs, restored it to its original purity. Offended by the novelty, I lent an unwilling ear, and at first, I confess, strenuously and passionately resisted. . . . With the greatest difficulty I was induced to confess that I had all my life long been in ignorance and error. . . . My mind was now prepared for serious attention, and I at length perceived, as if light had broken in upon me, in what a dunghill of error I had wallowed. With great fear and trembling at the misery into which I had fallen, and far more at that which threatened me in the prospect of eternal death, I could do no other than at once betake myself to Thy way, condemning my past life, not without groans and tears."

This is John Calvin writing to a cardinal six years after the All Saints' Day address of Nicolas Cop. Calvin is putting these words into the mouth of an imaginary convert to the Protestant faith, but they are words of his own experience, too. He was a man brought up in the church, working feverishly to find peace in other ways—in mastering studies, in writing a book, in becoming a humanist scholar. Finally, unwilling and stubborn, he is turned about in his way by God Himself. He is converted. Like Paul, he has come to his Damascus road.

"God by a sudden conversion subdued . . . my heart," says Calvin of himself in the preface to his commentary on the Psalms. "I was immediately inflamed with so intense a desire to make progress therein, that although I did not altogether leave off other studies, I yet pursued them with less ardor." It would seem, then, that this "sudden" turnabout must have taken place after the hard work on the Seneca commentary in which he scarcely had mentioned the Bible. It was most likely after the final months of study in Orléans. Perhaps the light broke in upon Calvin while he lived in the House of the Pelican with his devout landlord de la Forge.

Whenever it happened, this much was certain: John Calvin, the priest-to-be, the lawyer, the secular scholar, was gone. In his place now stood John Calvin, servant of Jesus Christ.

9

From the November day he left Paris in his vinedresser's disguise, Calvin had been wandering. First he had gone quietly to Noyon and stayed there a few days. But Margaret, the king's sister, had heard of his near capture. She persuaded the king, who was back in Paris, to show Calvin mercy. The hunted man slipped back into Paris and was received graciously in an interview with Margaret. Probably he stopped to see de la Forge and then left the city again.

He went now to Angoulême, to the home of a friend and classmate, Louis du Tillet. Du Tillet was a canon in the cathedral there, but he was sympathetic to the ideas of Lefèvre. He lived in a large house and had inherited from his father three or four thousand books, a fine library for those days.

Here Calvin was welcome, and here he stayed for some months under an assumed name. He had at least nine such names which he used at different times in different places. In the home of du Tillet Calvin called himself Charles d'Espeville.

Du Tillet's library was an ideal study retreat. Calvin began to study full time in the faith whose light had broken in upon him. Happily he hid himself here, writing to his friend François Daniel in Orléans, "I have learned from experience that we cannot see very far before us. When I promised myself an easy, tranquil life, then what I least expected was at hand: and, on the contrary, when it appeared to me that my situation might not be an agreeable one, a quiet nest was built for me, beyond my expectation, and this is the doing of the Lord, to whom, when we commit ourselves, Himself will have a care for us."

But the man under an assumed name was not left alone in his quiet nest. Educated men, welcome in du Tillet's house, searched him out to talk with him. God Himself drove the wanderer out of his study into the countryside, into the homes and villages of the common folk. The thin man in black slipped in and out everywhere. He held meetings secretly in homes. He gathered his eager listeners together in a little grotto near the river. People sought him, disregarding their own safety to hear the words of this hunted man.

In April of 1534 Calvin went to see the old professor, Lefèvre, whom he had never met. Lefèvre was in his native land again, in Nérac, a town under the protection of Margaret, Queen of Navarre. Lefèvre was almost a hundred years old. The last edition of his French Bible had just been printed.

Now there stood before him this young man, not quite twenty-five, already known as a leader of those who returned to the Scriptures. Both the old man and the young man loved their native France. Both of them had been born in the province of Picardy, known for its courageous, free-thinking people. The old man had been the first leader of the French Reformation. He had chosen to lead along peaceful lines, staying within the Church of Rome, hoping to achieve a reformation from within. Some say that in his last years the old professor was sorry for this. They say that he told the fiery, young leader before him how impossible it was to oppose the Sorbonne and the church and the court, how hopeless it was to raise the Church of Rome from its decay and superstition and turn it again to the Word of God. Did he say to Calvin, "You will be an instrument in the establishing of the Kingdom of God in France"? Did he sense that the mantle of his leadership would fall upon the young man who had come to see him?

No one knows what they said as they sat together, the old leader about to die and the new one fiercely devoted to the faith he recently had found. Fresh from the interview, Calvin set out for Noyon. He had made his decision. Not for him the way of the old professor who vainly had hoped to change the church from within. For a new faith it must be a new church—no, neither the faith nor the church was new. The faith was old, older than the cross of the Lord. It had been lost and now was found again in the Word. And the church to be reborn must be like the church of old, too, like the early church after Pentecost, a church of Christ, according to the Word.

Two months before he turned twenty-five, John Calvin stood before the clergy of Noyon in the cathedral under whose shadow he had grown up. He told these astonished churchmen, many of whom had known him since childhood, that he was not about to become their priest, that he was giving up his benefice with its salary of corn and grain.

It was May 21, 1534. Noyon's most famous son went out of its gates for the last time, following the same road that had taken him as a boy to Paris. Not again would he walk that road or enter the house on the corn-market square.

He went on his way, without a home and without a church.

10

It was a year of wanderings, a year of being hunted.

Calvin was hunted as a heretic fit for the fire. In a very different way, he was hunted by people hungering for the truth he taught and preached. "God so led me about through different turnings and changes, that He never permitted me to rest in any place . . . ," wrote Calvin, remembering these months.

First it was Paris, after he had left Noyon for the last time. He could not stay away from the believers in the capital city. He knew their passwords and their secret meeting places. He was back again in the house of de la Forge, who feared for Calvin's safety. Guardedly he went in and out of the homes of the faithful, teaching them, encouraging them, strengthening them.

Calvin spoke in many secret meetings, meetings sometimes disrupted by the police. He, too, knew what it was to scurry down a back passageway, to leap through a window, to melt into the darkness, to escape the shot of a musket. In those days Calvin would say at the end of his messages, raising his hands to heaven, "If God be for us, who can be against us?" Those who did not escape the police, whose places were empty at the secret meetings because they were waiting in prison for their turn in the fire—they bore witness to the truth of these words.

Again de la Forge pressed Calvin to leave Paris. Your life is not safe here, he told him. All France needs you. The Protestants have no leader, and we depend on you. Go, before it is too late.

Still Calvin waited. The people in Paris needed him, too. There was also an appointment he had agreed to keep with a young Spaniard named Servetus. This Servetus, two years younger than Calvin, denied the Trinity of God and boldly claimed that he alone possessed the truth. He had come to Paris after failing to find converts for his ideas in the German states. Now he hoped to convince the Frenchman whom he was to meet.

Calvin kept his appointment. Disguised perhaps, he came to the house agreed upon. Impatiently he waited for the Spaniard. But Servetus did not come. Nineteen years later, in a Swiss city, Servetus appeared and faced the man he had promised to meet in Paris.

43

From Paris Calvin went on to other cities, first to the flat, heath country around Poitiers where he had friends. Here he talked and taught in a park and later in a secret cave by the light of torches. Here, it is said, Calvin celebrated the Lord's Supper for the first time, using a flat rock for a table. He did it simply, quoting the words of Christ, without the pageantry of the Roman Catholic mass. From Poitiers Calvin sent out his first home missionaries, three men to preach and teach wherever people were waiting to hear.

But the police were closing in again, informed of the man in black who lodged in the city. Calvin escaped to Angoulême, to the home of his classmate du Tillet. Again people found him and pleaded to be taught. "All my retreats were public schools," said the man who called himself shy and bashful.

Next he was in Orléans, where he had studied law. There he finished the first published writing after his conversion. It was a little book written in Latin, with the imposing title *Psychopannychia*. In it Calvin had written against those who believed that the soul sleeps after death until the last judgment. The soul is alive and awake, claimed Calvin, even though it has left the body. In Orléans Calvin also wrote two prefaces to the French translation of the Bible completed by his cousin Olivétan. This intense, Christian writing was the work of the new Calvin, utterly different from his scholar's words on Seneca.

About this time big bundles of posters arrived secretly in Paris and in other French cities. The posters, written in French, protested against the Roman Catholic mass. On the morning of October 18, 1534, the posters appeared mysteriously in many public places. There was even one in the king's bedroom, in the container that held his majesty's handkerchief. Rumor was that the red-bearded reformer Farel had written them in Switzerland where he was now working. The language was angry and defiant.

King Francis, whose name was mentioned on the posters, rose up to take revenge. The Church of Rome was beside itself with rage. The Affair of the Placards, as it was called, filled the prisons. Smoke went up from the burning bodies of men. A new torture was used, a whipping gallows adjusted to lift the victim in and out of the fire, roasting him slowly instead of burning him all at once. Nowhere in France was a Protestant safe.

John Calvin, still looking for peace in which to study and write, rode east toward the German border and the Rhine. With him, on horseback, accompanied by two servants, was Louis du Tillet, who had decided to leave his work and his leather-bound books to go with his friend.

The friends rode east toward Metz, two hundred miles from Paris. It was winter, bitter weather with a stinging wind. At every inn where they spent a night, the travelers wondered whether someone would discover them and turn them in as heretics. Calvin traveled with two other constant companions, headache and an upset stomach. Besides all this, the friends got up on a certain morning to find that one of the servants had stolen their money pouch. The thief had escaped on his horse, leaving his masters penniless. They could not ask for money without making themselves known. The other servant, a better sort, loaned them enough to get them across the border to Strasbourg, where Calvin had friends among the Protestant ministers. Pastor Martin Bucer was there, helping the French refugees who were fleeing persecution in their own land. Calvin had written him before on behalf of one of these refugees.

Perhaps it was not peaceful enough in Strasbourg. Calvin and du Tillet pushed on to the south. There is a story that Calvin stopped on his way to see the Dutch scholar Erasmus. Erasmus was the man who had recovered the New Testament for the world by editing a new edition of the Greek text. But this great scholar who "paved the way for the Reformation discovered that out of the egg which he had laid, an entirely different bird had been hatched by Luther and Zwingli." Erasmus then retreated from the rediscovered faith and made his peace with the pope who offered him a cardinal's hat for his change of heart. He would be known in history as a humanist scholar, formally attached to the Church of Rome. When Calvin stopped to see him, Erasmus was old, forty years older than Calvin, and only a few years from death. How did he receive the young French leader who stopped to see him?

Early in 1535 the friends on horseback came to Basel, the Swiss center of learning and printing. Here, for more than a year, their wanderings ceased. Calvin had found a retreat at last. In a home in the suburbs he rented a room from Madame Catherine Klein, closed his door, and went to work. He took the name Martianus Lucanius, a name strangely like Luther's, the last name an altered spelling of Calvinius, the Latin form of his own name.

Only a handful of people knew who Lucanius really was. One who knew was Nicolas Cop, the former rector, now in Basel. He had not seen Calvin since the day that Cop was warned on his way to the palace and Calvin slid down the rope of bed linens to escape the bailiffs at his door. Far from Paris they now shared the news of the fierce persecutions in their native land.

The news was heartbreaking. A timid prisoner, to save his life from the fire, had pointed out the homes of those who attended the secret meetings. The wrath had fallen on them, though they probably had not posted the defiant placards. De la Forge, that pious, generous man whose house was a refuge for believers, had died in the fire. His wife was in prison. Calvin could not picture the House of the Pelican without these dear friends. The paralyzed shoemaker Milon had been tossed into the cart that took him to his death by slow roasting. Calvin knew him well—the man who could not walk but earned his living by making shoes for other folk to walk in. Du Bourg, a rich merchant who had been in the secret meetings, was dead, too. And so was Poille, the mason, who had his tongue fastened to his cheek with an iron pin because, as he came to the stake, he would not stop talking about his Saviour. There would be many empty places in the secret meetings of Paris.

King Francis was no longer fickle in his attitude toward the Protestants. The pleas of his sister Margaret ceased to move him. But he was kind enough to release her three ministers from prison and send them to a monastery. There two of them repented of their Protestant convictions and returned to the Church of Rome. The third, Corault, a man half blind, somehow escaped and made his way to Basel. Here he found Calvin and told him more of what was happening in Paris.

It seemed that King Francis found it helpful to tell a gross lie about his persecutions. He was clever enough to see that other countries, especially the Protestant states of Germany, would be angry at him for his cruelties. He needed these countries as his allies against Emperor Charles of Spain, who had beaten him at Pavia. So Francis wrote the German princes, explaining that the men he threw into prison and fire were only the worst kind of rebels, troublemakers, Anabaptists who wanted to split apart the church and state.

Were they rebels and troublemakers—the generous de la Forge, the paralyzed Milon, the others whose faces Calvin knew, and all the rest whom he remembered as brothers in the Lord? No one in France could speak for those in the fire. No one there could tell the truth about the faith of the martyrs. But a Frenchman in exile could speak.

The Frenchman lodged with Madame Klein in Basel sat down at his writing table and dipped his quill into the inkhorn. Feverishly he worked to finish the writing he had already begun. It was late summer when he wrote the letter dedicating it. Adding the letter to the six finished chapters, Calvin went off to his friend Thomas Platter, the printer whose shop was at the sign of the Black Bear.

11

The man to whom Calvin's book was dedicated never read the twenty-one-page letter addressed to him. "To his most Christian Majesty, Francis, King of the French and his Sovereign, John Calvin wisheth peace and salvation in Christ." So, in Latin, began the letter. But "his most Christian Majesty, Francis," was busy with his mistresses and balls, with his schemes to make alliances against his enemies. Perhaps he might have read the letter and the chapters that followed it, had someone told him that four hundred years later this book would still be counted among the handful of books which have shaped the thought of the world. King Francis could not guess that the letter addressed to him would be regarded as a masterpiece of burning eloquence and would be read by millions in many languages.

The *Institutes of the Christian Religion* by John Calvin of Noyon did not start out to be a plea to the king of France. It was meant to be a help to new Protestants who needed to be shown the truths of the Bible. No one of the Reformation had set these truths down on paper in an orderly way. Luther's contribution had been the translation of the Bible into German, and he had written other things on various subjects. The Church of Rome had its version of the truth. The people of the Reformation had the Word, but who was to lead them carefully into understanding it as a whole? Who was to show them what it said about God and Jesus Christ and the Holy Spirit, about the sacraments and the church, about faith and prayer, about the law and liberty in the Christian life?

Such a handbook, a little book, the Frenchman hiding in Basel was preparing when the news about the fiery death of his friends reached him. Then came news of the lies of King Francis. With a sudden flash of purpose Calvin saw how he could defend before the world the true faith of the people falsely accused. He saw too how he might move even the heart of the sometimes fickle king. The book became more than a study guide. It became a masterful confession of faith—the faith being sealed with the burning flesh of the martyrs of France.

"When I began this work, Sire," says Calvin to his king, "nothing was farther from my thoughts than writing a book which would afterwards be presented to your Majesty. My intention was only to lay down some elementary principles by which inquirers . . . might be instructed in the nature of true piety. And this labor I undertook chiefly for my countrymen, the French, of whom I apprehended multitudes to be hungering and thirsting after Christ, but saw very few possessing any real knowledge of Him. . . . But when I saw that the fury of certain wicked men in your kingdom had grown to such a height as to leave no room in the land for sound doctrine, I thought I should be usefully employed if in the same work I delivered my instructions to them, and exhibited my confession to you, that you may know the nature of that doctrine which is the object of such unbounded rage to those madmen who are now disturbing the country with fire and sword. . . .

"Wherefore I beseech you, Sire—and surely it is not an unreasonable request—to take upon yourself the entire understanding of this cause which has hitherto been confusedly and carelessly agitated, without any order of law, and with outrageous passion rather than judicial gravity. Think not that I am now meditating my own individual defense in order to effect a safe return to my native country; for, though I feel the affection which every man ought to feel for it, yet, under the existing circumstances, I regret not my removal from it. But I plead the cause of all the godly, and consequently of Christ Himself. . . . It shall be yours, Sire, not to turn away your ears or thoughts from so just a defense. . . . This is a cause worthy of your attention, . . . worthy of your throne. . . .

"What shall I say more? Review, Sire, all the parts of our cause and consider us worse than the most abandoned of mankind unless you clearly discover that we thus 'both labor and suffer reproach because we trust in the living God,' because we believe that 'this is life eternal to know the only true God and Jesus Christ, whom He hath sent.' For this hope some of us are bound in chains, others are lashed with scourges, others are carried about as laughing-stocks, others are cruelly tortured, others escape by flight. . . ."

With the keen mind of a trained lawyer, Calvin proceeds to list and argue each charge laid against the Protestants. He quotes abundantly from Scripture. He quotes from the church fathers. Sometimes his language is cutting and strong. He is pleading with the king, but he pleads for the truth and is not afraid to use firm language.

"We are peaceable and honest," he says of himself and those in France accused of being troublemakers. "Even now in our exile, we cease not to pray for all prosperity to attend yourself and your kingdom." We have learned "by divine grace" to be more patient, humble, modest. If some of us should use the Gospel as a "pretext for tumults," you have the laws by which to punish. But do not then blame the Gospel of God.

51

"Sire, . . . we despair not of regaining your favor, if you will only once read with calmness . . . this our confession, which we intend as our defense before your Majesty. But, on the contrary, if your ears are so preoccupied with the whispers of the wicked as to leave no opportunity for the accused to speak for themselves, and if those outrageous furies, with your connivance, continue to persecute with imprisonments, scourges, tortures, confiscations, and flames, we shall indeed, like sheep destined to the slaughter, be reduced to the greatest extremities. Yet shall we in patience possess our souls and wait for the mighty hand of the Lord, which undoubtedly will in time appear and show itself armed for the deliverance of the poor from their affliction, and for the punishment of their despisers, who now exult in such perfect security. May the Lord, the King of kings, establish your throne with righteousness, and your kingdom with equity."

These are some of the eloquent sentences that Francis, king of France, never read.

In the years that followed, the book grew. Usually called the *Institutes,* it grew like a plant from seed. In four editions, Calvin enlarged it from six chapters to eighty, filling four great books. There was nothing in the eighty chapters that had not been in the seed of six chapters. The sick man of fifty years, who later struggled to finish the final edition, interpreted the Word no differently from the young man of twenty-five hidden in Basel.

In its last edition of 1559 the *Institutes* followed the order of the Apostles' Creed to discuss the "truths of the Christian religion." Three of the four editions were in polished Latin. One was in vivid, beautiful

French. Today the *Institutes* can be read in at least ten languages.

So appeared the mighty writing which gathered together from God's Word a complete system of doctrine. The *Institutes* began with God and ended with God and found all things in God, the triune God. Calvin wrote clearly, with a lawyer's logic. He wrote eloquently, as an author who expertly wields his words. He wrote brilliantly, with a rare mind that grasped the whole of God's truth as man can know it. He wrote passionately, with a heart devoted entirely to his Lord. And he wrote humbly, because his soul had been delivered from the mire of sin only by the grace of God.

No one had so written before. No one has written since in any way approaching the magnificence with which Calvin set forth the "truths of the Christian religion."

But John Calvin of Noyon did not know of this success. He preferred, even in the days of the first, small edition, to stay out of sight, behind a closed door, under an assumed name. "That my object was not to acquire fame, appeared from this, that immediately after this I left Basel, and particularly from the fact that nobody there knew that I was the author."

Madame Klein's roomer, Martinius Lucanius, had spent much time at the shop with the sign of the Black Bear. He was reading final proofs on the book whose title page said in Latin, "John Calvin of Noyon." It was February 1536. When the proofreading was finished, before March when the book appeared for sale at the bookstalls, Lucanius and his companion du Tillet were gone from the city. On the highway south of Basel, Lucanius became Charles

53

d'Espeville, a name which means City of Hope. Du Tillet became Louis de Hautmont, which means High Mountain.

Mr. City of Hope and Mr. High Mountain were on their way to have a look at Italy, the land of the pope, the seat of the Church of Rome.

12

In a castle in the north of Italy lived a French woman who would have been ruler of France if the law had not said that the throne was for men only. Daughter of King Louis XII, the princess Renée had been engaged to Emperor Charles of Spain and then to Henry VIII of England, both times for political reasons. For the same reason she later had been given in marriage to an Italian, Duke Hercules of Ferrara. Hercules was closely related to the Church of Rome. He was related too closely, in fact, being a grandson of a pope.

The duke brought his French duchess home to Italy in a grand procession of scarlet pages and golden bugles. Though his enormous castle in Ferrara showed signs of crumbling and mildew, the life at the court there was gay and extravagant, an endless round of balls, banquets, and plays. Dwarfs, monkeys, and parrots added to the color.

Duchess Renée took with her from France a faith

that did not please her duke. She had learned it from the old professor, Lefèvre, from her cousin Margaret, and from others. At first the duke tolerated it, and he did not oppose the presence of Frenchmen in his court. But the Church of Rome soon pointed out to him his duty. These Frenchmen were the enemies of the pope, following the Protestant heresy. They had no business in the castle of a pope's grandson.

Duke Hercules was beginning to clamp down on his wife's friends when the travelers from Basel arrived at the walls of Ferrara. They came disguised as monks, it is said. Duchess Renée welcomed them eagerly. Perhaps her secretary, a poet named Clement Marot, had told her about the young leader of French Protestants. Marot had been number seven on the suspect list in Paris during the Affair of the Placards and had fled to Ferrara.

Now that Calvin had come, the duchess would need to protect him against the Inquisition, which already had begun to question some of her friends. The story goes that Calvin secretly met the duchess and her ladies-in-waiting in a little chapel next to the room assigned to him. Perhaps he brought along some proof sheets of his *Institutes*. If he was careful, he could talk with others in the court.

When Calvin came to Ferrara, the duchess was only twenty-four years old. Ahead of her lay dark years. She would be pressed to return to the Church of Rome. Refusing, she would be put into prison. Her children would be taken away from her to be reared in the faith of Rome. She would make herself appear obedient to Rome for the sake of returning to her family. After the death of Duke Hercules, she would go to her castle in France to make it a hospital and haven for the persecuted Protestants there. In the French religious wars to come, her own son-in-law would lead the troops against the Protestants. But she would remain steadfast in her faith.

Through all of this trouble ahead, the duchess' faithful counsellor would be the young man in black, who was now encouraging her at the court of Ferrara. She would never see John Calvin again, but his comfort and encouragement would help her to be true to the faith. By means of letters, often smuggled into the castle or the prison, the duchess heard from her spiritual advisor.

Twenty-eight years later, on his deathbed, Calvin dictated his last letter to the duchess, then living in her castle Montargi in France. She was concerned that the Protestants would blame her for being the mother-in-law of the man who fought them bitterly. "No, Madame," wrote Calvin reassuringly, though his own voice was almost too weak to dictate the words, "they only love and respect you the more, seeing that connection did not turn you aside from making an upright and pure profession of Christianity, and that not only in words but by deeds so remarkable. . . . As for myself, I . . . hold your virtues in so much the greater admiration."

But all this was hidden in the future. Now, in 1536, Calvin was speaking with the duchess in person. He wished that he could speak to others in high places in Italy. But he was prudent enough to see the threatening priests and cardinals all around him, and he did not go farther into Italy. His plan had been to come to Ferrara to strengthen the duchess, who was both French and Protestant. He had hoped she would be able to use her influence on those around her. He had even hoped the way would be open for him to speak and preach. But it was not. In the castle stronghold of Duke Hercules, too, the noose of opposition was being tightened.

During the six or eight weeks he was in Ferrara, Calvin sent out some letters. One was written to Gerard Roussel, a preacher whom Calvin had known and respected. King Francis had rescued him from jail and put him in a monastery with Margaret's other two preachers. Corault, the half-blind one, escaped to Basel, but Roussel confessed his "heresy" and returned to the Church of Rome. For this the pope offered him the mitre of a bishop and Roussel accepted. Calvin could not resist writing him.

"John Calvin to a former friend, now a Prelate," he addressed the new bishop. "What happens to one who like you deserts his captain, runs over to the enemy and destroys the ground for the defense of which he swore to give his life? . . . It is hard—how well I know—to leave one's home in order to become a pilgrim. And yet the Lord transforms this destiny, which in the eyes of men is so harsh, into sheer joy. . . ."

The pilgrims at Ferrara left suddenly. Duke Hercules was weeding out the heretics in his court, and suspicion had fallen upon Charles d'Espeville and Louis de Hautmont. These two escaped out of the city gates. Some say the thin, black-cloaked one preached on the way north to the Alps, and that he was welcomed in some villages and chased out in others. No one is certain what happened on this journey. Probably the travelers went by way of the Saint Bernard Pass. The mountain streams, swollen with melted snow, were leaping and crashing in their rocky beds.

And where to, now?

News came that King Francis, hoping to convert some Protestant heretics, had offered six months' freedom from persecution so that Protestants in exile could return to their homes and to the Church of Rome. Calvin made use of the opportunity. He crossed France and entered Paris. Remembering the friends who would not be there to greet him, he must have entered the city sadly. He took a room in a hotel. The House of the Pelican belonged to others now.

In Paris, on June 2, 1536, it is recorded that there appeared before two notaries ". . . Jehan Cauvin, Licentiate in Law, in person, and made his brother Antoine, clerk, living in Paris, his general and special attorney." John Calvin, possessor of a degree in law—how else would he describe himself to the notaries? As a wanderer, a heretic preacher, a Protestant writer? John Calvin, "Licentiate in Law," was making brother Antoine his attorney to act for him in the settling of the family property in Noyon.

Calvin also discussed the matter with his favorite stepsister, Marie. His other stepsister, faithful to the Church of Rome, had married and settled down in Noyon. Charles was dead, excommunicated from the church, buried at night in an unmarked grave at a crossroads outside the city.

The family of Gerard Calvin had come to nothing, said the townspeople of Noyon. That family once had been so respected, so faithful to the mother church. The innkeeper's daughter had died too early to keep her children in the way of the church. The clergy's attorney had become stubborn in his dealings with the churchmen. He had died that way, without making his peace with the church. His son Charles, the priest, had been an unruly sort. Once he had hit a mace-bearer in an argument over his father. Worse than this, Charles had turned away bitterly from the priesthood and gone over to the "Lutheran heresy." On his deathbed, and he so young, he would not take the sacrament. Buried in unholy ground he was, his soul not blessed by the church. And the next son, good in his studies, the one who started out to be a priest, too—this John was turning out to be the worst of them all. He could write and he could talk so that people would listen to him. He taught heresy. He wanted to start another church, against the holy mother church and the pope. Someday he would burn for his wickedness—either in the fires of France or in the fires of hell itself. It was a terrible thing he was trying to do. And John was turning the minds of his younger brother Antoine, the clerk who worked in Paris, and of his stepsister Marie. They were going to follow John wherever he went. So said the other stepsister, the faithful one, the only one of the family who had not turned out badly. The pious women of Noyon shivered when they passed the Calvin house on the corn-market square. To what an end that family had come!

John, "the worst of them all," was on his way across France again. The king's six months of mercy would end soon. There was no quiet place in his native land where he could hide behind a door and a false name, as he had done in Basel. Such a hiding place he needed again, to study and to write. That would be his contribution to the new Protestant faith—writings and books from which men could learn and take courage. Perhaps Strasbourg would be a good retreat this time. Or Basel again.

Strasbourg lay east, but to go that way was to walk straight into the path of a war. King Francis was having his third war with Emperor Charles. They were fighting in the area Calvin would have to cross to go directly to Strasbourg. Cannon and carts and other military equipment clogged the roads. So Calvin made a large detour, passed through Lyons, known for its hundred printers, and approached Strasbourg from the south. He had hoped to get as far as Lausanne on a certain day. Failing this, he decided to spend the night in Geneva on the west end of Lake Léman.

Tired and dusty, he came to the old Cornavin gate, guarded by a sentry in armor. Calvin gave the sentry his name, received a paper recommending him to the landlords of Geneva's inns, and crossed the drawbridge into the city. He was weary and aching. But after a little food and a long sleep he planned to continue his journey north at daybreak. He found an inn and asked a night's lodging.

Part II
Man of Two Cities

13

The bravest people in all Europe lived in the mountains and valleys of Switzerland. It was not called Switzerland at the time of the Reformation. Instead, it was a group of thirteen states, called cantons, which had won their freedom from the dukes, kings, and emperors who ruled the other peoples of Europe. Each canton ruled itself by councils of citizens. Nowhere else in Europe did the people rule as did these uneducated but unbeatable folk, who would not be servants to any master.

Soon after 1500 the Swiss cantons faced a great question. What would they do with the Reformation? This movement was sweeping the German states and had begun at the same time in their own cantons. Up in the middle north Ulrich Zwingli was preaching mightily in the Grossmünster church of Zurich. He had preached his first sermon there on New Year's Day 1519, fourteen months after Luther hammered up his theses. From this beginning the Swiss Reformation spread to other cantons. In the north and east, the German-speaking cantons were debating whether they would stay with Rome or become Protestant. Some declared themselves faithful to Rome. Others turned to the faith preached by Zwingli and Luther. Because in those days church and state were still tied together, a canton either became officially Protestant or remained officially Roman Catholic.

In the north, the most powerful Protestant canton was Bern. Bern had the figure of a bear on its official seal, and all the cantons knew that when the Bern bear roared, it was wise for them to beware.

Protestant Bern began to do mission work in the lands and cities under its control. This was not easy because the Church of Rome was ready to fight to the death for the areas it still held. The people of Bern were German-speaking. They needed someone to be their missionary in French-speaking territories of the southwest. So they sent a Frenchman, the fiery, red-bearded William Farel. Farel had been converted under the old professor, Lefèvre, and had escaped from France after hard work in Meaux and Paris.

William Farel was as daring a missionary as ever carried the Word to new places. He stopped at nothing. "Never in my life have I seen so bold a man," said Erasmus of the stocky, red-bearded man who, in turn, had called Erasmus a Balaam. Once, as a religious procession passed, Farel pulled some relics from a priest's hand and threw them into the river. Other times he entered a church of Rome, climbed the pulpit, and outshouted the priest who was intoning the mass. Wherever he went, he stirred up a storm. In one town after another, in the market place, in homes, in halls, he thundered his message. He could whip his audiences into a fever of excitement. With shouting and scolding and whispering and groaning, with common, biting language, he sent his arrows into the hearts of the sturdy, uneducated folk who flocked to hear him. He was unrefined just as they were, and they could understand his kind of talk. He roared against Rome. He proclaimed the truths of the Bible with such eloquent sincerity that people were moved either to believe at once or to attack with fury the missionary sent by Bern.

Beaten and trampled upon in some towns, Farel was threatened with pistols and swords in others. Once he was scratched so severely that a man from Bern who saw him reported that the missionary's face looked as if many fierce cats had dug their sharp claws into it. But Farel never stopped. Nor was he very careful to stay within Bern's territory. If a field was unharvested for the Gospel, he arrived there, whether Bern could protect him or not.

Farel trained a handful of fearless men to help him. They were not afraid of hunger, cold, death, or any man. If they were not driven out, they stayed long enough in a town to convert some people to the Reformation. Then they sent notice to Bern, whose council wrote the town asking that a public debate be held between Protestants and the Church of Rome. Bern would send officials to take charge of the debate, and at the end of it the people would vote, choosing for the Reformation or for Rome. Many towns and villages declared themselves for the Reformation. To such places Bern would send rules about the sacraments and worship. The mass would be abolished. Statues and altars would be taken from the churches if they had not been knocked down already by overenthusiastic Protestants.

It was on an autumn day in 1532, exactly a year after Zwingli had been killed, that Farel and a companion missionary crossed the drawbridge into Geneva for the first time.

John Calvin was in Orléans, France. He was finishing his course of law, after the poor sale of his book on Seneca.

14

Few cities had as beautiful a location as did Geneva. Built on the rock beside a blue lake, it grew within a circle of mountains, some green, some snow-capped and wrapped in clouds. The blue lake gathered up the waters that flowed down from the mountains and sent them on in a mighty river, the Rhone, which went rushing on its way into France and the Mediterranean. Geneva stood at a crossroads of Europe. Important trade routes passed through her gates. The city was in the very southwest tip of the Swiss cantons, looking out on the countries around her.

Julius Caesar in his famous marches through Europe had discovered Geneva fifty years before the time of Christ. He had built walls of defense there. Four hundred years later Geneva had become a city. By that time Christianity had come to change the pagan community. In place of heathen temples, churches had been built. Beginning in the tenth century, the impressive stone cathedral of Saint Pierre was built atop the highest point of the city. It was shaped like a cross, and its square, fortress-like towers stood out against the mountain backdrop.

Geneva was still struggling for her freedom when Farel paid his first visit to the city. She belonged to no canton and was fighting desperately to become an independent city. For one hundred fifty years Geneva had been carving out more power for her citizens, defying the clutch of bishop and duke who wanted to rule the city. But it was a bloody fight.

Duke Charles III of Savoy ruled the lands around Geneva. The castles in the area were his strongholds. He had even captured the castle on the island in the middle of the river between the two parts of the city. The bishop ruled the citizens as head of the church to which they all belonged. He was the enemy inside the city until he moved away to a more comfortable palace on a mountainside. The duke was the enemy outside.

The patriots of Geneva fought bitterly against the duke. Finally, in 1525, Duke Charles besieged the city with a great army. The patriots fled as he triumphantly entered the gates, and the men who were left gave their oath to bow to the duke. What else could they do while the duke's soldiers held long-handled axes over their heads? But the patriots returned. They met in council and cast aside the pledge to the duke. Stunned by the sudden opposition, he unexpectedly fled from Geneva without a battle and was never able to enter the city again.

Geneva now turned to the strong cantons of Bern and Fribourg and made alliances with them. The alliance of 1526 was adequate for maintaining freedom from the duke. But Bern was Protestant while Fribourg was for Rome. When the battle in Geneva became one also of religion, the city on the lake again stood alone.

Farel entered this Geneva in 1532. He took a room in the inn Tour Perce and quietly made known his arrival. The next day he spoke to a group gathered in the inn to hear him. The second day he preached to a crowd. By this time the nine hundred priests of Geneva had leaped into action. They knew well enough what damage the daring missionary had done to the Church of Rome in other places.

Because he carried safe conduct papers from Bern, Geneva's ally, the city councils could not put Farel out of the city. So the priests gathered a mob and closed in on Farel and his companion as they walked through the streets. Hissing and shouting, carrying clubs and spears, the attackers would have killed the traveling missionaries if a troop of town soldiers and officials had not arrived to break up the riot and to escort Farel and his friend to the inn. A guard stood at the door of their room all night. Early the next morning, friends took Farel and his helper across the lake in a boat and put them ashore in a secluded spot.

William Farel was accustomed to such receptions. He made a new plan for Geneva. Within a few weeks notices were posted in the city. People read with interest, "A young man just come to this town will give instruction in the reading and writing of the French language, to all who will, big and little, men and women, even to those who have never been to school. If within a month they cannot read and write, he wants no money for his trouble. He is to be found in the Great Boytel-Hall, near Molard Square, where the Gold Cross hangs out. He also cures many sicknesses for nothing."

Soon the rented room at the sign of the Gold Cross was full of pupils. The teacher, a young man of twenty-one, was Antoine Froment, secretly one of Farel's helpers. He taught the French he had promised, but with it he generously mixed small sermons and comments on the Bible.

The room overflowed. People flocked to hear the young teacher. On New Year's Day of 1533 the crowd was so large that Froment was rushed off to Molard Square, a common meeting place for the citizens. Here he stood on a fish stall in the open air of winter and preached to the people on the text, "Beware of false prophets."

He was still preaching when an angry mob, led by armed priests, descended on Molard Square. Froment escaped into the house of an apothecary whose windows were soon smashed for sheltering the teacher. Like Farel, Froment left Geneva in a hurry, hidden by the blackness of the night. But the seed the two Frenchmen had planted took root and grew.

Now the fight over religion really began. Protestant Bern moved into the battle with a letter to the councils of Geneva, "Let truth, your Excellencies, have free course." Within the city the people were divided.

By torchlight seven hundred priests, canons, and other followers of Rome met and pledged themselves with an oath to kill every Protestant in Geneva. The next day they gathered in front of the high altar in Saint Pierre. Canon Wernli led them, dressed in a suit of armor. While the great Clemence bell pealed, the army of seven hundred marched out of the cathedral with banners, crosses, swords, axes, spears, and clubs. Down through the streets they marched to Molard Square, joined as they went by reinforcements. Women appeared, their aprons loaded with stones. Teen-agers joined the ranks. All lined up in battle array and waited for the fight to begin.

The Protestants, too, gathered their forces in the large home of one of their number. Five deep they came out to meet their fellow citizens. With weapons poised, both sides faced each other across the square. And then, amazingly, seven visiting merchants from Fribourg stopped the fight before it began. They stepped between the two sides and begged them to make peace instead of fighting, neighbor against neighbor. The priests were hard to convince, but at last the armed folk went home. For five weeks there was an uneasy peace.

Once again, on a late afternoon in May 1533, Canon Wernli laid aside his robes and buckled on his sword and armor. Followed by armed priests, he arrived at dusk in Molard Square. The news spread through the narrow streets. The alarm bell rang and frightened everyone. Protestants and followers of Rome rushed out to join the fight. In the darkness Canon Wernli swung his sword left and right through the crowd. There was a short tussle, a few men were wounded, and then the fighters retreated into their houses. All except Canon Wernli, whose body was discovered the next morning. He lay dead on a doorstep, a slim spear thrust deep between the joints of his armor.

This meant more trouble. Canon Wernli was of a noble family in Roman Catholic Fribourg. The council of Fribourg demanded the punishment of all who had sided against the canon. Kill them, said Fribourg, or we will break our alliance with your city. But then the Bern bear stepped in. It, too, was in the three-way alliance.

We are greatly troubled by your treatment of the Protestants in your city, said Bern to her little ally Geneva. You have thrown out of your city "our servant, Master Guillaume Farel." You have caused trouble to our servant Froment. You have invited into your cathedral a professor from the Sorbonne in Paris who "preached only lies, errors, and blasphemies against God, the faith, and ourselves, wounding our honor, calling us Jews, Turks, and dogs." We will not suffer it. We are sending a delegation to Geneva to meet with your councils and to arrange a public debate for all the people to hear.

Thereupon the Council of Bern sent back its redbearded bachelor missionary to preach and to take part in the requested public debate. Farel reappeared in Geneva in December of 1533, carrying the collapsible pulpit he set up wherever he wished to preach. Froment, the teacher, was also back in the city. And a third preacher, a native Swiss, arrived. This one, Peter Viret, was a learned and lovable man, much respected wherever he went. In his back he carried the scar of a lance wound inflicted by a priest.

The councils of Geneva were being squeezed to a choice. If they refused to arrange a public debate, the delegation from Bern threatened to tear the seal from its alliance with the city. If the councils agreed to hold the debate, it would help to establish the Reformation in Geneva.

Meanwhile the number of Protestants was growing. For a time Farel had preached in a large house which could hold four hundred people. Then the Protestants had marched in a multitude to take possession of the Convent of the Rive which could hold five thousand. Viret baptized converts and spoke against the priests' order that all copies of the Bible were to be burned.

Finally the councils agreed to a public disputation in Saint Pierre. It lasted a week and was a victory for the Protestants. But before the Protestant cause could be put to a vote of the citizens, the Duke of Savoy reappeared outside the city. He had made an agreement with the much-hated bishop. Fribourg had torn the seal from its alliance with Geneva. Bern was standing back, unwilling to become involved against the duke who was backed by Emperor Charles V and the pope. Geneva was now in real danger.

The duke's castles around Geneva were full of armed men. He sent an ultimatum to the councils of the city. Get rid of the three preachers, the duke ordered. Take back the bishop, become again an obedient child of our mother church, and I will not send my armies to destroy you.

Bern sent its advice to the little city. It would be wiser for you to submit to the duke than to be crushed, said Bern. The Swiss cantons met and sent their advice to the councils of Geneva. Submit, said the cantons. You cannot stand against the duke, the bishop, the pope, and the emperor.

The people of Geneva saw clearly what the duke's ultimatum meant. It was not so much a matter of religion. It was the choice between liberty and bondage. To live under the tyranny of the duke who had allied himself with the bishop and with Rome— could Geneva submit to this after fighting long and bitterly for her freedom?

The councils gave their answer. They spoke the mind of the people. *We will not submit,* said Geneva to the duke and his allies. We would rather be buried beneath the ruins of our city than lose our liberty.

15

It was August of 1534 when the citizens of Geneva decided to tear down the four suburbs of the city that lay outside the wall. They did not want the duke's army to have any place in which to take cover as it approached the city. This meant sacrificing half of the city to save the other half, since six thousand people lived in the shady suburbs. Day after day the people pulled down the houses and villas, the churches and monasteries. They used the stones to repair the walls. The church bells were melted and made into cannon balls. Leaving a wide demolished area around them, the citizens of Geneva crowded within the walls of the half city that was left. All winter they worked to make their defenses more secure. The men built with the dirt and stones which the women carried to them. Farel and Viret were up on the ramparts with the people, encouraging, standing night watches, and sharing the work.

In April 1535, someone tried to poison the preachers. Viret became very ill. The maid in the house where the preachers stayed confessed that she had put poison in their spinach soup. Farel had been called away before he ate the soup. The maid was tried and put to death by the councils. Priests were blamed for bribing the maid. In the tense, crowded city this brought a strong reaction in favor of the preachers.

Meanwhile, the duke was sniping from near by. He began to cut off the supplies coming to the city. He captured citizens who ventured outside the walls and carried them off to his castle dungeons for torture or death. Still he did not send his full army.

In June a second public debate began in Saint Pierre. It lasted four weeks. People crowded in to hear the preachers defend the Protestant faith against two monks who turned up late to speak for the Church of Rome. The monks were no match for the preachers, and the people cheered for the Protestant cause. On Sunday, August 8, 1535, with a great demonstration, Farel was carried up the street to Saint Pierre. People stood massed in the doorways and overflowed into the square outside while Farel preached the first Protestant sermon from the cathedral pulpit.

The next day Farel was called before the councils. He pleaded to have the Protestant faith formally recognized. Gladly will I and my fellow preachers submit to death at your hands, said Farel, if it can be proved that we preach anything contrary to the Holy Scriptures. Then he knelt down and prayed with the councils. The room was quiet as he rose from his knees.

The councils also invited representatives of the Roman Catholic priests and clergy to speak for their faith. But these men were slow in coming. When they did appear, they seemed careless and unenthusiastic. One said frankly that they considered themselves unlearned men, teaching whatever their fathers had told them.

With this evidence before them, the councils of Geneva made another momentous decision.

By an edict of August 27, 1535, the religion of Rome ceased to be the religion of Geneva. The mass was celebrated no more. Statues and altars which had not been knocked down already were carried out of the churches. One monastery became a free elementary school which children had to attend. This school was the first of its kind in all of Europe. Another monastery was turned into a hospital.

Priests, monks, and nuns were given the choice of staying in the city or leaving it. Many chose to leave. The nuns of the convent of Saint Claire seem to have feared they would be forced to marry if they stayed in Protestant Geneva. So they left, too. But some of them had not been outside their convent for thirty years. They had a terrifying trip through the hills where they thought every sheep or ox was a hungry bear or lion.

And so the Reformation came to Geneva hand in hand with the freedom which no citizen of the little city would surrender. The duke had forced the decision more quickly. Since he stood with the bishop and the pope, those who cherished freedom leaned toward the three preachers and the Protestant faith.

Now the duke set up a full blockade with his ships on the lake and his army encircling the city. Crowded inside the walls of Geneva, the people saw starvation approaching. Somehow a messenger got through the duke's blockade and carried a pleading letter to Bern. While the council of Bern sat arguing the matter, word came that the duke's soldiers had plundered some of Bern's districts in the Geneva area.

To protect its own rights, Bern sprang into action, declared war on the duke, and marched toward Geneva with six thousand Swiss fighting men. Even King Francis of France jumped into the affair and declared war on the duke. Francis captured the duke's capital city and two of his richest provinces while the duke was away at Geneva.

It was February of 1536 when the troops of Bern arrived at the gates of Geneva. The city on the lake was saved!

Farel began to introduce new worship and preaching and rules into the newly Protestant city. The councils called the people of Geneva to the cathedral of Saint Pierre. They stood, all together, and swore with hands raised to heaven that they would live according to the laws of the Gospel, forsaking the ways of Rome. It was Sunday, May 21, in the year 1536.

The year 1536. . . . In it the Dutch scholar Erasmus died at Basel, having pointed the way to the Scriptures and then turned back from following in that way. In the French town of Nérac died the old professor, Lefèvre, the "morning star" of the Reformation, who had lived more than a century in a troubled world. It was the year when England's Anne Boleyn, the second queen of Henry VIII, lost her head on a chopping block in the Tower of London. It was also the year when a young traveler had to make a detour on his way from Paris to Strasbourg. He stopped to sleep one August night in the city of Geneva, which was still recovering from its struggle against the duke.

The traveler came to stay a night. He planned to leave, unnoticed. But God planned otherwise.

16

Two men were arguing. The older one, stocky and short, did most of the talking. He stood, he sat down, he paced the floor. He waved his arms, and he pounded his fist on the table. He poured out his words in a torrent that could not be stopped. He spoke in a roar. He spoke in a hoarse whisper.

In a chair sat the other man, the younger one, thin and pale, with piercing eyes that shone out of his bearded face. He shook his head. He raised his hand to interrupt. When he found a break in the older man's stream of words, the younger one protested. I cannot do it, he said. It is not for me. I am shy and timid. I am afraid in the face of trouble. Besides, I am often sick. A study is the place for me. I am a man of books and of writing. How can I bind myself to one church if I am to serve them all? You cannot ask it of me. "In the name of the Lord," have pity upon me and allow me "to serve God otherwise."

The candle on the table burned lower. Still the

men argued. Finally the older one, pointing his finger to heaven, thundered, "I say to you in the name of the almighty God, to you who only put forth your studies as a pretense, that if you will not help us to carry on this work of God, God will curse you, for you will be seeking your own honor instead of Christ's!"

The man of the piercing eyes bowed his head. Silence hung in the room. The argument was over. "I felt . . . as if God from heaven had laid His mighty hand upon me to arrest me. . . . I was so stricken with terror, that I stopped from the journey I had undertaken. . . . William Farel detained me in Geneva." The traveler, John Calvin, had agreed to stay.

What did the bold, fiery Farel want with a sickly man only twenty-seven years old? Farel, who was used to taking people and cities by storm—what did he need from this shy man twenty years younger than he?

No one could conquer a city for the Gospel like William Farel. Once he had conquered, the work was just begun. Next came the careful planning, the firm leading, the building up. For this work Farel was not the man. No one knew that better than he. He was magnificent in a battle. But he was quite lost in the day-to-day planning and strengthening. He could not give the firm, steady leadership which an explosive city like Geneva needed.

Already the Reformation in Geneva was having its troubles. The people who had sacrificed everything rather than submit to the duke were turning back to normal living again. Many returned eagerly to the wild living for which their city had been well known. They were quite ready to forget the Protestant faith, which had arrived along with the fight for freedom.

While the duke had been at the gates of the city, everyone had united in a common cause. Now the different groups were bobbing up again, hating each other, scheming how to control the councils. There were the new Protestants. There were the leftover followers of Rome. And there were the people who called themselves the real patriots. The patriots were not pleased with having imported French preachers to run the new Protestant church.

In the middle of all this emotion, Farel and his helpers were losing their hold. The people did not relish enforced laws about how to behave. Formally, they all were now members of the Protestant church. But how many of them there were with hearts unchanged! And what would happen to this newly Protestant city if someone did not mastermind the plans to turn the rebellious city into a city of God?

It was du Tillet, the friend of Calvin, who told Farel that Calvin had come to spend a night in Geneva. Suddenly Farel saw the answer to his problems. Here was a Reformation leader, a brilliant young man, a man whose training in law equipped him to deal with the councils as well as the factions in the city. Above all, here was a man who comprehended as no other man of his day what the Bible taught. This man could teach the Word to others. With the help of the Spirit, he could change the lives of the citizens of Geneva. Calvin was God's answer for Geneva's need. Farel had no doubt about it. At top speed he had set out through the narrow streets to the inn where Calvin was lodging.

And now Calvin had agreed to stay. He told the

brethren in Geneva that he must first go to Basel to bring a relative on his way and to pick up a few of his own belongings. He would stop at some churches as he went. In a few weeks he would be back in Geneva to stay.

Calvin kept his promise. But, "as soon as I got back to Geneva," he wrote a friend in France, "a violent cold attacked me, which afterward settled in the upper gums, so that there was scarce any relief even after nine days, and this after having been twice bled, with a double dose of pills and several poultices."

All this was not a very glorious introduction to Geneva. Calvin got up from his sickbed to begin his work with daily lectures in Saint Pierre. His title was dignified enough. Professor of Sacred Letters, he was called. But he was a professor without pay. In September of 1536 Farel asked the city council to employ Calvin as a teacher of the Scriptures and to pay him for his work. The council employed him but took until the following February to get around to paying him anything. Meanwhile Calvin was listed in the council minutes only as "that Frenchman." Either he was quite unknown or the council clerk did not understand his name.

Every afternoon Calvin climbed the steep little street that led to the cathedral. Here he lectured in the huge auditorium, stripped bare of its images and altars. A small group came to hear what he had to say on the epistles of Paul. Besides his studying and correspondence, he was working on a French edition of his *Institutes*.

Calvin was also brooding with a sadness that bordered on anger. All around him the people of Geneva were plunging back into the life they had given up while they fought the duke. The taverns were always full. Drunken folk staggered through the streets. The dice rattled merrily in the gambling contests. The card games never stopped. Men made no secret of their mistresses or their use of prostitutes. Platforms were set up in the town squares for a great season of dancing. To Calvin the clothing of the people seemed gaudy and immodest. Men were wearing slashed breeches instead of modest robes. Women flaunted their silks and jewels in daring fashions.

All this in a city which had formally declared itself for Protestantism! Many of these were the people who had raised their hands solemnly in Saint Pierre, swearing to live by the Word of God. They all belonged to the church of Geneva. How could a refugee Frenchman, a stranger among them, begin to teach them the faith they did not know? How could he lead them into a life of consecration so different from their daily wickednesses?

Perhaps the text of Calvin's underground days in France came back to him with comfort in these months: "If God be for us, who can be against us?" Who, indeed?

17

Late in September of 1536 Calvin and Farel made a journey eastward around the lake to Lausanne.

Here they met Viret, who was now pastor in that city. Bern was sponsoring a large public debate in Lausanne. The debate was intended to settle the matter of religion in the surrounding territories which Bern had conquered from the duke. More than three hundred priests of these territories had been invited. Of the one hundred seventy-four who arrived, only four priests stood up to speak in the debate. Farel and Viret were to be the speakers for the Protestant faith. Calvin went along, but he did not expect to take part.

The people of the newly conquered territories left their farms and villages. They overflowed the inns of Lausanne. It would be up to them to vote on their religion, and they did not want to miss this chance to hear the arguments on both sides.

The beating of drums announced the beginning of debate on October 1. Farel opened it with a Sunday sermon. On Monday at seven in the morning the debate was continued. People crushed against each other in the cathedral to see and hear. The contestants sat in the center of the church. To make the debate official, five deputies from Bern sat there, too, wearing black doublets, red hose, and wide-brimmed, feather-trimmed hats. Secretaries had their quills ready to record the debate.

Farel presented ten theses for debate, and the arguments continued for a week. On one of the days a speaker for Rome was talking about how the body of Christ is really present in the Holy Supper. He accused the Protestants of ignoring the ancient church fathers on this point. If you knew what the fathers have written, said the speaker for Rome, you would see your views stand condemned.

This was too much for Calvin. All the hours he had spent studying the church fathers while a student at Paris now came to his help. He rose and began to refute the speaker for Rome. With magnificent memory he quoted from Cyprian, Tertullian, Chrysostom, Augustine, and many others. He not only quoted by author. Calvin identified the book or writing in which the church father had written. All this he presented in flawless argument. When he had finished, the great crowd stirred with excitement. People pushed for a better look at the pale young man they did not know.

A Franciscan monk cried out that this was the true doctrine. He called on God to forgive him for following the teaching of Rome so long. Many others agreed with him, though they did not cry out. In the months that followed, one hundred twenty priests and eighty monks in the areas around Lausanne turned to the Protestant faith, which had become the official religion of those territories.

Next Calvin was off on horseback to Bern, still nursing his cold, which did not improve in the sharp October winds. In Bern the question was how to unify all the little Swiss parishes instead of letting each one wander into its own interpretations of the new Reformation faith. Calvin was becoming better known. People saw in him a leader. Even the folk of Geneva turned out in large numbers to hear him when he returned to the city he now called home.

And now to the building up of the church of Geneva. At his table in the dark little house near Saint Pierre, Calvin dipped his quill into the inkhorn and began writing.

The first result was a *Confession of Faith.* Through

its twenty-one articles Calvin meant to make clear to the people of Geneva what it was they had promised to uphold when they swore allegiance to the Gospel. In November of 1536 the *Confession* was brought to the councils, who received it for study. The preachers asked that the people should swear to live according to the *Confession*. Some councilmen complained that people should not be forced to swear to something they did not believe. But in the end the thing was approved.

In every district of the city, street by street, house by house, the captains of the districts assembled their people and marched them up to Saint Pierre. They came by tens and stood before the secretary of the council. He was in the pulpit, recording the names of those who took the oath. Day after day the people came and took their oaths to be faithful to the truths of the *Confession of Faith*.

But not everyone would come. The mutterings grew louder. Did we fight against the duke and the bishop only to be slaves to the preachers within our walls? asked the discontented. Who gave these Frenchmen power over us? The leftover followers of Rome stirred up the people. The lovers of loose living, called Libertines, complained because they saw that the preachers meant to make them live by the *Confession*. The patriots fumed at what the foreigners were doing to control the city.

Meanwhile, from the pen of Calvin came another careful document. In their black robes, Calvin and Farel brought it to the town hall. Guarding the council door was a herald sitting on a wooden lion and holding a silver-topped staff in his hand as a sign of authority. He would admit the preachers to the meeting of the Little Council, the first of Geneva's governing councils. On the Little Council of twenty-five men sat the four syndics, the most important officials of the city, elected by the people. There was next the Council of Two Hundred, whose members were elected by the Little Council, and who, in turn, elected the Little Council members, except for the four syndics and the city treasurer. The third council was the Council of the Whole. All the male citizens of Geneva were its members, and they were called together on matters of the greatest importance.

So the black-robed preachers presented Calvin's handwritten document to the Little Council. In it the preachers requested that four reforms be made in the church of Geneva. "It is not possible to reduce everything to good order in a moment," said the document, "if only because the ignorance of the people would not allow it. . . . But now that it has pleased the Lord a little better to establish His reign here, it seemed to us good . . . to confer together concerning these things . . . praying you in the name of God that . . . if . . . you see that our advice is from the holy Word of the Gospel, take good care that these observations be received and obeyed in your city. . . ."

We will study it, said the Little Council. It was mid-January, 1537. People were still being gathered by tens in Saint Pierre to swear allegiance to the *Confession*. And the thin young Frenchman whom Farel had commanded to stay in Geneva had not yet been paid a penny for his services.

18

Well, what do the preachers want now? asked the Little Council, taking from its table the document addressed, "Right Honorable Gentlemen."

The right honorable gentlemen did not have far to read to find the dynamite in the document. "It is certain that a church cannot be . . . well ordered . . . unless in it the Holy Supper of our Lord is always being celebrated . . . and this under such good supervision that no one dare presume to present himself unless devoutly, and with genuine reverence for it. For this reason, in order to maintain the church in its integrity, the discipline of excommunication is necessary."

Excommunication. So this was the idea—to give the church the mighty weapon of excommunication which the pope so long had brandished in fearful fashion. Through faithful men on watch in every quarter of the city, the pastors proposed to have reports of those who did not live the life of Christ. It would then be up to the church to take the steps Christ sets forth in Matthew 18. These would end in excommunication, a decision of the church which the councils would enforce, since the church and state in those days were tied together. This "discipline of excommunication is necessary," said the preachers, in order to keep wicked hands from the sacred table of the Lord. But this was the dynamite—to let the church have this power of excommunication, and that for wicked living as well as for believing false doctrine.

Shall we have a new pope within our walls? We will do the punishing in Geneva, shouted many of the council members. This is our power. We have books full of laws that can be used to punish the wicked. Let the preachers preach and teach. Let them leave the lives of the citizens in the hands of the councils who are called to rule the city.

Calvin not only asked that the church be allowed to decide who might partake of Communion. He also believed that the Lord's Supper should be celebrated more often. "It would be well to require that the Communion of the Holy Supper of Jesus Christ be held every Sunday, at least as a rule. . . . It was not instituted by Jesus for . . . two or three times a year, but for a frequent exercise of our faith. . . . Such also was always the practice of the ancient church . . . ," he pointed out. "But because the frailty of the people is still so great, there is danger that this sacred . . . mystery be misunderstood if it be celebrated so often." So let it be celebrated "once a month."

The other three reforms did not stir up such a tempest in the councils. Calvin asked that the laws about marriage be studied and set up anew, according to the Word, since "the pope has so confused" them "by making decrees at his pleasure." In this sentence in the document there was a blank space left in place of the pope's name. Calvin would not honor the pope by so much as writing his name.

"The third article concerns the instruction of

children, who without doubt ought to make a confession of their faith to the church." They must be taught by a catechism. And this "is more than ever necessary now, in view of the neglect of the Word of God which we see in most people, and the contempt of parents in instructing their children in the way of God." For this a catechism must be written. Parents must teach it to their children. And "at certain sessions of the year," the children must come before the ministers to be asked these questions and to have them explained further. "May it be your pleasure to command parents to exercise pains and diligence that their children learn this summary," pleads Calvin.

One more new thing. "There are the Psalms which we desire to be sung in the church." If this reform is adopted, the people will sing in church. They have not sung there for centuries. They have not even understood the Latin words sung and chanted by the priests. Now, instead of being dumb spectators, they will have a part. By such singing "one may pray to God, or . . . sing His praises . . . and render thanks to God with one accord." How will the people learn the Psalms? Let "children, who beforehand have practiced, . . . sing in a loud, distinct voice, the people listening with all attention . . . till all become accustomed to sing communally." The children as a choir will lead in teaching the new tunes. There will be no organ, no harmony, only sturdy, unison singing.

This was John Calvin's four-point plan for beginning to build up the church in Geneva. It was a plan in which he believed. It was a plan patterned after the early church. Was it a plan the councils would approve?

The councils dragged their feet. They did not decide against singing psalms, teaching children, and setting up marriage laws according to the Scriptures. They could lay these reforms on the law books of the city along with a hundred other laws that were not being enforced. That would satisfy the persistent preachers.

But this business of excommunication and the Lord's Supper. On this there were many furious arguments. The weight of the councils was against any change. Let the celebration of the sacraments go on as now, four times a year, instead of every month or every week. And let the whole matter of excommunication be laid aside. After all, no other Reformation church in Switzerland had such power in its hands. Freedom-loving Geneva need not give in on this point, either—especially not to satisfy a foreigner!

The preachers did what they could with this lukewarm reaction. Calvin wrote a catechism for children, to help parents teach them the truths of God's Word. He was preaching now, too, his clear, metallic voice piercing to every corner of the churches in whose pulpits he stood.

Calvin also was becoming well known in the city streets. He and Farel, with their flat black caps bobbing, went calling in the homes. Sometimes the old blind preacher Corault went with them, walking more slowly, tapping his stick on the cobblestones.

Everywhere the preachers walked, the sins of the people rose up to taunt them. Loaded dice and dirty packs of playing cards were always in motion. In the noisy taverns men tossed off tankard after tankard and came reeling into the streets, ready for a wild night of brawls and cursing. Prostitutes flirted in broad daylight. And what went on by night—!

Yet these people, every one of them, belonged to the church of Geneva. They were its members because their city had declared itself Protestant. What could a preacher do with such a congregation of twelve thousand people?

How could Calvin bring into the lives of these rebellious folk the faith and life of which he had written brilliantly in his *Institutes?*

Well, he could preach the Word, couldn't he? And preach it he did. Looking down into the sea of faces below the high pulpit in Saint Pierre, he stretched out a long bony finger and laid the sins of the people upon their hearts. He minced no words. Farel did not mince any words either as he thundered forth to the people gathered in the church of Saint Gervais, across the river from Saint Pierre. Corault was in the pulpit of another church, preaching with fire to people his eyes could not see.

And the ministers could push the councils to enforce the laws of the city. They beat a path to the door of the council chamber, demanding that the laws lying idle on the books be put to work. There were hundreds of such laws. Each city of that day had detailed laws about the private lives of its citizens.

There were laws about everything. There were even laws about such things as what time people had to go to bed, what kind of wedding dress a bride might wear, how many musicians might be hired for a party, and how many numbers they might play. Some of the punishments were severe—prison, banishment, even death.

Interestingly, a good number of these laws had been placed on the books before the Reformation ever came to Geneva. Farel had persuaded the councils to add others early in 1536, during the first enthusiasm over Protestantism.

But the laws had no teeth in them. Like the laws of many other cities, they gathered dust until the preachers pounded on the council door and demanded action. They were asking action against any offender, whether he was rich or poor.

19

Meanwhile two Dutchmen came to town and added to the trouble of Geneva's pastors. They were Anabaptists, these Dutchmen, and they asked for a debate with the preachers. The Anabaptists believed, among other things, that all Christians who turned from Rome to the Protestant faith had to be rebaptized. In Reformation times they had the reputation of being the radicals among the new Protestants. Luther opposed them vigorously. They often preached revolution and violence. In Geneva such topics were explosive. During the two days of debate before the Council of Two Hundred, the preachers refuted the Anabaptists vigorously, and the council ordered the Dutchmen out of town. But they had stayed and talked long enough among the people to add fuel to the fires of discontent, which were spreading in Geneva.

Next came the brilliant Caroli with his wild charge that Calvin and the preachers of Geneva did not believe completely that Jesus is God. Caroli was then pastor in Lausanne, eastward around the lake from Geneva. He had come to Protestantism from the Church of Rome. Already he was leaning back toward Rome, praying for the dead and preaching other doctrines in that direction. He also had a history of loose living, for which Farel and Viret had denounced him when he was in Geneva in 1534. In Lausanne with his usual bold talk he had convinced the city council that, since he had a doctor's degree, he should be made senior pastor over the veteran reformer Viret, who had been in Lausanne before him. Now Caroli made his attack on the doctrine of the Genevan preachers.

That he should be accused of not believing in the Trinity roused Calvin to white heat. It was a preposterous charge, as could be seen by anyone who had read his *Institutes* and his *Confession of Faith.* "Never have I heard anything so outrageous," wrote Calvin to his friend Megander. Enraged, he went up to Lausanne to defend himself and his colleagues at a synod there. The Geneva ministers replied to Caroli in strong language. Calvin spoke in a fury. When he had finished he was exhausted, coughing, and out of breath.

The synod decided in favor of Geneva's pastors. Later a synod at Bern put Caroli out of the Protestant ministry because of his immorality. He returned to France and to the Church of Rome. But his wild words hung like evil rumors among the Swiss churches. The common folk heard and wondered what was going on among the ministers of the new Protestant church. Deeply bothered by this, Calvin urged that another synod be held in Bern to bring about a common declaration of doctrine. "The peasants object," he wrote, "that we ought to be agreed among ourselves before we endeavor to bring others to be of our mind. . . . We must lose no time" in setting up a synod "where all controversies of this sort are to be decided."

Caroli had done his damage. Farel was completely upset, though he was usually a man to stand up well in the thick of a storm. Calvin wrote to Viret in Lausanne, pleading with him to come back to Geneva to help. "I consider your being restored to us to be indispensable," he wrote, "unless we are willing to lose Farel, who is more exhausted with the great anxiety than I ever thought would be the case with one of such an iron constitution."

In the same letter to Viret, written in Latin, Calvin wrote, "Mr. de Hautmont intends returning to France. . . . Will you send back the cloak and such of the books" as are his?

These words meant that Calvin was also losing a friend in the middle of all his troubles. Mr. de Hautmont was Louis du Tillet, the faithful traveling companion who had left his large library and his work in Angoulême to travel with Calvin out of France, to Basel and to Italy. He was the one who told Farel that Calvin had come to stay one night in Geneva. Du Tillet had stayed with Calvin in Geneva. He had watched the storms gather around his friend. He had seen Calvin sick and angry and upset and despondent. The troubles of Geneva were no pleasure to du Tillet's mild disposition. He began to wonder. Was *this* the true church of Christ that his friend was attempting to set up in all the rebellion and wild living of Geneva? Or was the true church the mother church of Rome? Perplexed, du Tillet talked of returning to France.

But when he did leave, du Tillet left secretly and went north to Strasbourg on the Rhine. Here he took refuge again in the Church of Rome. Before he crossed the border into France, he wrote some letters and sent them by messenger to Geneva, to tell his friend Calvin what he had done. Are you convinced in your heart, wrote du Tillet to Calvin, that you are lawfully called of God to be a minister in the Protestant churches? Is this the true church of Christ?

Before the messenger arrived with the letters, Calvin had heard a rumor of what his friend had done. After reading the letters, he picked up his pen to answer. He wrote without anger, with respect, love, and sadness. But he also wrote firmly.

I have missed you, he wrote. And "what troubled and tormented me most was the fear" that in "such rudeness and incivility as I used towards you" at times, I should have offended you and driven you to your decision. Yet I am sure that my rudeness has not been the cause of your change of heart, for which I have you to thank, rather, "than because I conducted myself as became me."

But "I have been very much astonished on hearing of your intention," continued Calvin. "This so sudden change has appeared very strange to me, seeing the constancy and firmness which you showed." I cannot share with you the arguments you advance. But "I will make no long dispute." Let me thank you for your gracious sharing with me of all you had. "Would that it pleased God I could make you a due acknowledgement. . . . Have special remembrance of us in your prayers, . . . as the difficulties which press upon us are now greater than ever. . . . I pray the Lord to keep you in His holy protection, and so to direct you that you may not go astray in that slippery path whereon you are. . . . Your very humble servant and brother, Charles d'Espeville." So wrote the honest man in Geneva, who confessed his own faults while he also clung with conviction to what he believed. In all this he clung also to his friend.

Du Tillet was gone, not only in miles but also, it seemed, from the faith. Farel was still beside himself. The people of Geneva in their elections of February 1538 had put into office three syndics who were enemies of Calvin and his reforms. The Council of Two Hundred had ordered the preachers not to exclude anyone from the Lord's Supper. The Little Council, on a flimsy pretext, had thrown out some of its members who were sympathetic to Calvin. When the preachers arrived at the council chamber to protest this, they were told to go home. Stick to your preaching, said the council, and do not meddle any more in the politics of the city. We will not admit you here again.

Now came a request from the canton of Bern, whose Protestant and political influence was heavy in all the districts around Geneva. Bern asked the councils of Geneva to adopt certain rites for the churches of their city. (Farel had put aside these and other church practices when he first came to Geneva, because he wanted to be done with everything that smacked of the Church of Rome.) We ask you to use

95

baptismal fonts in your churches again, said Bern, and also to use unleavened bread, such as wafers, in the Lord's Supper. Besides, let us all observe Christmas, Easter, Ascension Day, and Pentecost as holy days. It is good for all the churches to be alike in these things. What Bern did not say was that it asked these things in order to draw Geneva under its political influence, too.

Agreed, said the Council of Two Hundred to the requests of Bern. The Bern church rites were adopted by the council without consulting the preachers in whose churches the rites would be used.

On a Saturday morning the blind Corault mounted his pulpit for the six o'clock service. The week before he had been ordered not to preach again because he had spoken angrily against the council for deciding matters of the church. But here he stood again, still denouncing the council for its action. "My lords the governors are like the image of Daniel, with feet of clay," he cried. "They are like rats among the straw." Before he could finish, the soldiers of the council reached him and took him off to prison. It was the day before Easter.

Calvin and Farel pushed through the gathering crowd that hissed and spit at them. They climbed the steps inside the town hall and passed the herald at the council's chamber door. To the council they said, You have done wickedly in imprisoning a servant of the Lord. He spoke the truth when he preached that you have no right to decide the worship of the church without first consulting the church itself.

The council was uncomfortable under the wrath of the preachers. They bargained: We will wait to put the Bern rites into practice if you will agree to let us put Corault out of his office as preacher. To this we will never agree, replied the two men in black robes. Neither will be introduce the ceremonies of Bern. The city council has no right to impose these upon the church.

Outside the mob was waiting for the preachers. "To the Rhone, to the Rhone," shouted some, picturing the preachers sinking in the swift, icy currents. Others hurled filthy names at the backs of Calvin and Farel. More spitting, more hissing, more fists and sticks shaken within inches of the bearded faces. And when night came, more boots kicking at their door, more gunshots fired under their windows, more dirty songs sung raucously. Someone had even paraded up and down the streets, mocking the Lord's Supper with an obscene ditty, while the onlookers laughed gleefully.

This was all a nightmare to the shy twenty-eight-year-old Frenchman, at his desk with quill and flickering candle. He jumped with every shot and with every boot that kicked his door. The Lord had set him over a church instead of putting him into a quiet study. But what a church and what a city! How long would he be required to stand against the storm?

Saturday night. The people in the streets made way for the council herald with his silver-topped stick. Carrying a lantern, he came to the preachers' door by order of the syndics. Would the preachers agree to use the rites of Bern? If not, on order of the syndics, the pastors Calvin and Farel were not to mount their pulpits the next day. Other preachers would be found to preach the Easter sermons and to administer the Lord's Supper to the congregations.

Sunday morning. Easter Sunday morning. The

97

churches were full to overflowing. A rowdy crowd poured up the street to Saint Pierre to see what would happen. Across the river, where it was Farel's turn to preach, the church of Saint Gervais was also brimming over with citizens. Would the preachers preach? Yes, the preachers had decided to preach. After a sleepless night, they made their way to the churches— Farel across the river, Calvin a little walk up the narrow street to Saint Pierre.

Here Calvin stood, his bony fingers gripping the pulpit rail, his piercing eyes looking down on an angry, buzzing congregation of several thousand people. What a sermon he preached that Easter morning! Clearly, frankly, firmly he spoke to the people. How could they reach forth their hands to receive the bread and wine of the Holy Communion when they had sinned so stubbornly against the crucified Christ? Could the Holy Supper be celebrated in the midst of fighting and rioting? God forbid.

There was no celebration of the Holy Communion in Saint Pierre on that Easter Sunday morning. Nor in Saint Gervais across the river. Unharmed, the two pastors moved through the muttering crowds to their house.

At the Easter Sunday afternoon services the two preachers preached again. It was Calvin's turn to take the pulpit in the Church of the Rive, down by the shore of the lake. In ominous silence his audience waited. When Calvin in his convincing frankness spoke about the troubles in Geneva, men leaped up with swords flashing. Shouting and fighting, they pushed toward the pulpit. Friends of Calvin rushed to him and made a human shield around his body. "By a miracle," reported a witness, no blood was shed. The human shield escorted the preacher up the streets to his door.

Inside their house Calvin and Farel waited for the next move from the councils. They had not long to wait. Late on Sunday the syndics met in special session. On Monday the Council of Two Hundred gathered to make its decision. We give the pastors Calvin, Corault, and Farel three days to get themselves out of our city, said the council.

The herald with his silver-topped stick came to announce the sentence. Hearing it, Calvin replied, "Well and good. If we had served men we would have been ill-requited, but we serve a good Master who will reward us."

Three French pastors on rented horses rode over the drawbridge that crossed the moat, past the sentry in armor and out of the city gate. They were leaving Geneva—the old blind man just out of prison, the red-bearded one who was used to being thrown out of cities, and the thin, young one with the piercing eyes who had stayed twenty months instead of the one night he had planned.

It was April 25, 1538.

20

It is no light thing for a pastor to be put out of his church. Leaving the weak, blind Corault in a town where he had friends, Farel and Calvin rode on. They wanted to defend themselves before the city council in Bern and at a synod of Swiss churches in Zurich.

As they rode along in the spring air, Calvin and Farel had time to think. The sound of the mob was gone. Things looked a little different to them now. Had they been too quickly angry, too harsh, too stubborn over small things? They had no doubts about the faith they preached. Nor did they doubt the need for order in the church and for discipline in the lives of its members. But had they employed the proper methods to get these things established?

To the synod at Zurich, Calvin and Farel said that they would accept the church rites proposed by Bern. But, they said, we continue to believe that a city council should not decide such things about the worship of the church. They also explained their convictions about church discipline.

The Swiss churches wanted peace in their parishes. The synod hoped to have the ousted pastors reinstated, and Bern was asked to send a delegation to Geneva to arrange this. But the councils of Geneva had not changed their minds. They sent a herald to meet Calvin and Farel, who had begun their trip back to Geneva to be ready if peace were made by the Bern delegation. The herald carried a letter commanding the preachers not to re-enter the city.

Once more Calvin and Farel turned their horses away from the towers of Saint Pierre. What more could they do? This time they set out for Basel, the city which had been Calvin's quiet retreat while he wrote his first edition of the *Institutes*. It was a trip of more than a hundred twenty-five miles. The preachers reached this city on the Rhine by the end of May 1538.

The trip had not been easy. Calvin wrote his friend Viret in Lausanne, "We have at length reached Basel, but well soaked with the rain and completely spent and worn out. Nor was our journey free from perils, for in truth one of us was almost carried away by the swollen currents; but we have experienced more tender treatment from the impetuous river than from our fellow men. . . ."

The two bachelor preachers planned to stay together. But soon Farel was being urged to come to Neuchâtel, a town to which he had brought the Reformation. Calvin had letters from Strasbourg, asking him to come there. In July he went to visit the Strasbourg pastors. They begged him to become pastor of the French refugees who were arriving from the persecutions in France. But Calvin was not ready to take another church. He wrote from Strasbourg to du Tillet, the friend who had left him, "I shall retire to Basel, waiting to understand what the Lord would have me do."

But now Calvin was waiting alone in Basel. Farel, his closest friend, had listened to the pleas of Neuchâtel and had gone to be pastor there. Calvin soon wrote him the first of many letters. He told Farel about the trouble arising in Geneva over the appointment of new preachers. "But . . . ," he writes, "let us humble ourselves . . . unless we wish to strive with God when He would humble us. Meanwhile, let us wait upon God."

Two weeks later Calvin sent another letter to Farel. Calvin had risked his own life to help the dying nephew of his friend. "Last Sabbath-day your nephew

101

was seized with the plague," wrote Calvin to Farel. "His companion and the goldsmith who bore testimony to the Gospel at Lyons brought me word immediately. As I had taken some pills to relieve the complaint in my head, I could not go to him myself. . . . A woman was engaged to sit up with him. . . . She got her son-in-law to assist her. . . . I visited him as soon as my health allowed it. When signs of certain death appeared, I strove to give him medicine for the soul rather than for the body. He wandered a little in his mind, yet had so much consciousness of his state as to call me back to his chamber . . . to pray for him. . . . This morning, at about five o'clock, he departed to the Lord. . . . That excellent man, the goldsmith, because he had contact with the infected, has been dismissed by his master. I have sent him, with my recommendation, to Strasbourg, that he may get work there. . . . Concerning the wearing apparel and other movables of your nephew, thus you have it: . . . He has a sword and a shirt with Wolf [his landlord]. I know for certain that he had no money when he fell ill."

The money for the nephew's care and for his burial Calvin himself had provided, although he was selling part of his library to get money to live. Nor had he bothered to stay away from a man with the plague, though the goldsmith had been fired by his employer— so deadly and contagious was this epidemic. For the sake of helping the nephew of a friend, money and health were worth sacrificing.

Suddenly Calvin was in Strasbourg to stay. In early September 1538, less than five months after leaving Geneva, he arrived there from Basel. Earlier he had refused to hear the arguments of Pastor Martin

Bucer and his colleagues. But Bucer knew how to act the part of a Farel. When pleas brought no results, he threatened: "God will know how to find the rebellious servant, as He found Jonah." Calvin boarded a river boat and traveled ninety miles north down the Rhine to Strasbourg. "My departure from Basel was . . . hurried and disorderly," he wrote Farel. The hand from on high had been laid upon him. Again this hand did not lead him to a quiet study.

But the three years in Strasbourg were like a pleasant dream compared to the horrors of Geneva. Strasbourg was a city at peace. Its famous mayor, Jacob Sturm, was in favor of the Reformation, and he had set up many schools for children. The Protestant churches were at peace. They gave their members an orderly program of preaching, catechism, and sacraments. They even had a system of discipline and family visitation, though the councils of the city kept in their hands the power of excommunication.

On September 8, 1538, a few days after he had arrived in Strasbourg, Calvin stood again in the pulpit. The contrast to his last stormy church service in Geneva could not have been greater. Here he was in the little church of Saint Nicolas, near the south wall of the city and the meadows that stretched out beyond it. Before him were gathered some of the French refugees who had found safety in Strasbourg. Their faith was a treasure to them. Facing death in their native France, the refugees had fled to be true to this faith. Reverently, eagerly, they listened to the preacher who had come to preach to them in their own language. A month later Calvin wrote Farel, "For the first time, we have administered the sacrament of the Supper in our little church according to the custom of the place, which we purpose to repeat every month."

No more mobs and fights, no more shouts and shots beneath his window, no rebellious people appearing for the holy sacrament. Calvin walked the streets in peace. Through the city wound the River Ill, with footpaths on its banks and trees leaning over to be reflected in the smooth-flowing water. On one side of the river, high above everything, stood the magnificent Roman Catholic cathedral, a Gothic masterpiece of red sandstone with a lacy tower stretching four hundred sixty feet into the air. In the south transept of the cathedral was the giant astronomical clock. Famous throughout Europe, it told the position of the planets as well as the time of day. Each time it struck the hour, a gold figure representing one of the twelve apostles moved forward to strike a bell. And for Peter there was a small gold cock that crowed. The clock is there today.

Not far from the cathedral stood the smaller church of Saint Thomas. Dr. Martin Bucer was its pastor. His church was of gray stone, with a square, squat tower. Inside, the church had been stripped bare of images and altars to make it a place of worship for Protestants.

Calvin lived for a time in Bucer's home, which was near the church. He was not the only person who lived there, for the Bucer house was known as "the inn of righteousness." Many a refugee or traveler had warmed himself before its hearth and eaten bread at its table. Besides the stream of guests, Bucer had a family of six active children. His wife, Elizabeth, was as hospitable as he.

Calvin was now a pastor in the free German city of

Strasbourg. The Antioch of the Reformation, this city was called. What then had Geneva been—a Sodom?

21

John Calvin, at twenty-nine the pastor of the French refugee church in Strasbourg, had not only exchanged a Sodom for an Antioch. He himself seemed to have changed. He was less ready to fight, more ready to listen and to learn. His stay in Geneva apparently had not turned out for the success of the Gospel there. "Willingly, therefore, do we acknowledge before God . . . that our unskillfulness . . . deserved to be chastised," he wrote Farel from Strasbourg, still thinking of what had happened in the Swiss city by the lake.

In Strasbourg Calvin was willing to celebrate the Lord's Supper "according to the custom of the place." While he would not allow babies to be baptized by midwives because it was contrary to the Word, he did not raise his voice against things in the church which were not basic. "As to trifling ceremonies," he advised Farel, "strive to induce the brethren not to dispute the point. . . ."

With the students whom he taught, he saw to it that they did not take their swords to class. But he did not raise his voice against their clothes which he thought immodest. And he said tolerantly, "Nor ought . . . discipline to be stretched so far that they may not play the fool on some occasion."

Instead of the fuming Farel, Calvin now had Bucer for a senior partner. Bucer was almost as old as Farel, but he was a champion of peace and cooperation. In Strasbourg Calvin had no need to beat a path to the city council. He became a busy pastor, teacher, and writer.

Calvin found joy in his little congregation of French refugees. His preaching attracted French-speaking folk from all around. Carefully he went over the order of worship then used by Bucer. It came from Lutheran practice, and in some of it Calvin saw much good. What delighted him too was that the French refugees had been singing psalms in French for more than ten years. They sang enthusiastically. It was a thrill to hear them.

In 1539 Calvin published a songbook with eighteen psalms and the Apostles' Creed set to music. Some of the song texts were written by Calvin. The rest were the work of Clement Marot, the poet whom Calvin had met in 1536 at the court of Ferrara in Italy.

One by one Calvin was putting into practice the things he had wished to do in Geneva. In the spring of 1539 his French congregation voted to use a system of discipline like that of the other Strasbourg churches. The people were happy with their preacher. He went in and out of their homes faithfully. He cared for them, taught them, preached to them, and gave them the sacraments.

Besides this, Calvin was appointed "lecturer in Holy Scripture" in the Strasbourg Gymnasium, a secondary school that became one of the most outstanding in Europe. Its rector was the scholar John Sturm, formerly of Paris and a friend of Calvin. Besides teaching in the Gymnasium, Calvin agreed to give public lectures on the Bible, as he had done in Geneva. "I either lecture or preach daily," he wrote Farel.

Calvin was writing also. Down to the printer, whose shop was in a former convent, he brought the second Latin edition of his *Institutes,* a much larger work than the first one. This edition he also translated into French, into such fine French that Calvin later became known as the father of modern French, as Luther with his translation of the Bible is called the father of modern German.

In October 1539 Calvin's public lectures on the Book of Romans appeared in print. This was the first and one of the finest of his many commentaries. Calvin also wrote a small book on church worship. He explained what he believed to be the best order of worship according to the ancient church. He included a form for celebrating the Lord's Supper and a simple form for marriage.

And then he published his *Little Treatise on the Holy Supper of Our Lord,* which was not very little after all. It included sixty short chapters and was written in French instead of in scholar's Latin. Calvin hoped the common people would read it because no doctrine was as much argued about in those days as that of the Holy Supper. On this doctrine the followers of Luther, Zwingli, the pope, and Calvin never could agree, any one of them with any other.

Strangely, the pastor of the French refugees was now a member of the guild of tailors. One could not be a citizen of Strasbourg unless he belonged to such a trade guild, whether of butchers, cobblers, wood-workers, drapers, or some other trade. Wishing to become a citizen of the city, Calvin squeezed the twenty-florin fee out of his meager earnings. He applied at the guild hall of tailors, which was close to the hall where he gave his public lectures. Whether he had talent as a tailor or whether he chose that trade because its guild hall was close to his lecture hall—who knows? Whatever the reason, John Calvin was a citizen for the first time since he had left his native France.

But the busy man in the peaceful city also had his troubles and sadnesses. He was desperately poor. As in Geneva, the Strasbourg city council agreed to pay Calvin and then forgot to do so. When the council got around to it, six months later, it was at the rate of a florin a week, hardly enough to support him. To Farel he wrote, "Will you see that Balliot sends the money for the payment of Wendelin the printer? At present I can hold on no longer. . . ." And again, "Whatever shall remain due I will pay when able; for such is my condition at present that I cannot reckon a single penny my own."

Calvin and Farel still owed the man with whom they had boarded in Basel. The man sent a bill. It included the cost of wine, but there was question in Calvin's mind about whether the wine had been given by another friend as a gift. Yet the landlord had charged for it, and Calvin wrote Farel, figuring out his share in the bill. "I am unwilling to haggle about it. . . . You have boarded seven weeks and two days with him, myself two months and about twelve days. . . . Thus I divide it: I pay five gold crowns, you, four. . . . I yet owe you a crown and a half, which I will pay as soon as possible. . . . I have about twenty shillings of Basel money." Every coin counted, and Calvin had none to spare!

An offer of money came to the poor preacher. Du Tillet was writing from France, "It is possible that you may be ill-provided with money, without which you cannot live in a manner becoming you; but you need not mind about that . . . if you wish it, God willing, I will supply enough to meet your necessity."

In the same letter du Tillet suggested that Calvin return to France, hinting that Calvin might return to the Church of Rome. But Calvin replied that he was sure the Lord had led him to his Strasbourg work and to the Protestant churches. Not wishing to be obligated in any way by using his friend's money, he said politely, "You have made me an offer for which I cannot sufficiently thank you. . . . I shall abstain, however, . . . from being burdensome to . . . you, who have already in the past been put to too much expense."

Not long after this, a pious-talking swindler came to see Calvin. The man put on such a convincing Christian act that he persuaded the poor pastor to lend him twenty batzen, or about eighteen gold francs. Perhaps Calvin had to borrow some of the money in order to lend it. The swindler left him a little basket of his belongings as proof that he would be back soon to pay the debt. "When he returned a few months later," wrote Calvin in a letter, "he asked me smilingly, or rather, mockingly, whether I didn't want to lend him a few crowns. I answered that I was in need of the little sum which he had already had."

Without repaying the loan, the swindler disappeared. A year and a half later Calvin decided to open the basket that had been left with him. He called over his friend Sturm of the gymnasium and a few others. Together they lifted the lid and viewed the precious contents—some rotten prunes, some tattered clothes, some frayed books, and some letters which the man had stolen from others. "Not without much laughter" did we look at these things, said Calvin, who chuckled heartily despite the trick that had been played on him.

After living a while in Bucer's home, Calvin rented a house where he took in some students as boarders. Things were not always peaceful in the rented house. Sometimes the students failed to pay their landlord. Sometimes the housekeeper, a woman with a sassy tongue, caused an uproar in the place. Sometimes Calvin himself, tormented with a headache or an upset stomach, gave in to the temper he was trying to control.

Once Calvin reported to Farel that he had lost his temper completely. Who had turned up again but Caroli, the ex-preacher of Lausanne, who had accused the Geneva preachers of not believing in the Trinity. For the second time Caroli now announced himself converted from Rome to Protestantism. For the second time he left France and came to Switzerland and Strasbourg.

Calvin and Farel decided to forget the earlier trouble and, if Caroli's return to them was sincere, to receive him with love. But Caroli was quite ready to stir up past differences. In Strasbourg he tried to make Bucer and the other ministers suspicious of Calvin. The ministers and Caroli drew up some statements of doctrine, signed them, and sent them to Calvin late at night for his signature. In their eagerness to make peace, the ministers had agreed to some points of Caroli's thinking with which Calvin could not agree.

If he signed the statements, Calvin would be untrue to his convictions. If he refused to sign, Caroli would accuse him of deserting his friends and being a lone troublemaker. Upset, Calvin asked for a meeting of the ministers. They met for supper in one of the homes. And "there I sinned grievously," wrote Calvin to Farel, "in not having been able to keep within bounds; for so had the bile taken entire possession of my mind, that I poured out bitterness on all sides. There was certainly some cause for indignation, if moderation had only been observed in the expression of it. . . . I stated my resolution rather to die than subscribe to this. . . . At length I forced myself out of the supper room, Bucer following, who, after he had soothed me by his fair speeches, brought me back to the rest. . . . When I got home I was seized with an extraordinary paroxysm, nor did I find any other solace than in sighs and tears." Here was the servant of Jesus Christ, a human servant, struggling with his besetting sin, weeping bitterly when he had failed to control it.

There was more to weep about in Strasbourg. There were tears of sorrow, too. A month after Calvin came to Strasbourg, while he was still in Bucer's house, news came of the death of his blind companion, Corault. There was a rumor that Corault had been poisoned in the little town of Orbe where he had gone to be a minister. "The death of Corault has so overwhelmed me, that I can set no bounds to my

111

grief," Calvin wrote Farel. "None of my daily occupations can . . . engage my mind. . . . Distress and wretchedness during the day seem only to prepare . . . for the more painful and excruciating thoughts of the night. It is not merely the want of sleep, to which custom has so inured me, by which I am harrassed, but I am utterly exhausted by these melancholy thoughts all night long. . . . That atrocious deed . . . rankles my mind, if indeed the suspicion is well founded. . . . We, the survivors whom the Lord has left behind for a while, let us persevere in the same path wherein our deceased brother walked, until we have finished our course. . . ."

Not only Corault was gone from earth. In Italy at the court of the Duchess of Ferrara, Olivétan had died. He was only thirty-two years old. Over his death, too, hung the suspicion of poison. First a comrade preacher had died. And next a cousin from whom he had heard the truths of the Reformation in Paris, to whom he was attached by faith as well as by blood, for whom he had written prefaces to a French New Testament.

Fortunately, Calvin was not alone in Strasbourg. He had many friends in the churches and schools. He also had with him his stepsister Marie and his brother Antoine. Some years before these two had left Noyon, their birthplace, to be with their famous brother. They had lived for a time in Basel. Probably they had been in Geneva during the stormy twenty months. Now they were in Strasbourg. Calvin was glad to have them with him.

Yet the words of family-man Bucer kept popping up in his mind. You ought to have a wife, Calvin, Bucer had said.

22

"We look for the bride to be here a little after Easter," Calvin wrote Farel in February of 1539. "But if you will make me certain that you will come, the marriage ceremony might be delayed until your arrival. . . . I request of you . . . that you assure me that you will come. . . . I would rather have you than anyone else."

This wedding which Farel was asked to "solemnize and ask a blessing upon" never took place. There is no further mention of it, nor of the lady who was expected after Easter. Urged by his Strasbourg friends, Calvin again was thinking of marriage in May when he wrote Farel, describing the kind of woman for whom he was looking. "But always keep in mind what I seek to find in her; for I am none of those insane lovers who embrace also the vices of those with whom they are in love, where they are smitten at first sight with a fine figure. This only is the beauty which allures me, if she is chaste, if not too fussy or fastidious, if economical, if patient, if there is hope that she will be interested about my health."

February 1540 and the preacher is still unmarried but hoping. "In the midst of such commotions as these," he writes Farel, "I am so much at my ease as to have the audacity to think of taking a wife. A certain

113

damsel of noble rank has been proposed to me, and with a fortune above my condition. Two considerations deterred me from that connection—because she did not understand our language, and because I feared she might be too mindful of her family and education. Her brother, a very devout person, urged the connection. . . . His wife also. . . . When, thereupon, I replied that I could not engage myself unless the maiden would . . . apply her mind to the learning of our language, she requested time for deliberation."

It seems that the maiden's uncertainty about learning French warned Calvin not to consider her further. "Thereupon," he continues, ". . . I sent my brother, with a certain respectable man, to escort hither another, who, if she answers her repute, will bring a dowry large enough, without any money at all. Indeed, she is mightily commended by those who are acquainted with her."

This eligible one had a dowry of virtues rather than of cash value! "If it come to pass, as we may certainly hope will be the case, the marriage ceremony will not be delayed beyond the tenth of March. I wish you might be present, that you may bless our wedlock. As, however, I have troubled you so much more than I ought during the past year, I dare not insist upon it. . . . I make myself look very foolish if it shall so happen that my hope again fall through."

Once again the hope did fall through. Calvin did not wish to enter this marriage. On March 29 he wrote to Farel, "We are as yet in a state of suspense as to the marriage, and this annoys me exceedingly." The lady was pressing for the marriage, but Calvin had heard some things about her. "Unless the Lord had altogether demented me," I would not marry her, he now says. "But because it is unpleasant to refuse, especially in the case of such persons, who overwhelm me altogether with their kindness, most earnestly do I desire to be delivered out of this difficulty."

Calvin was on the spot. How did one courteously get rid of a woman one did not wish to marry? Brother Antoine, who had helped arrange this romance, was given the job of ending it. Considerably embarrassed, Calvin resolved to think carefully before he fell into such a predicament again. June came and he was saying, "I have not yet found a wife, and frequently hesitate as to whether I ought any more to seek one."

Then came August 1540, and Calvin was married. Farel came from Neuchâtel to perform the ceremony. Calvin had found a bride in his own congregation of refugees. Once having found her, he did not wait long to marry. The bride was a widow with two children. Besides having all the qualities that Calvin had listed in his letter to Farel, she was also quite beautiful.

Idelette de Bure came from what is now the Dutch province of Gelderland. Her first husband, a tradesman named Jean Stordeur, had been converted from his Anabaptist views by Calvin's preaching in the refugee congregation of Strasbourg. Soon thereafter Jean Stordeur had died of the plague.

Calvin could not have asked for a better wife than the new Madame Calvin. But from the beginning of her marriage to the French preacher, the good woman never had her husband wholly to herself. It was not easy to enter Calvin's student boardinghouse and to put up with the sharp tongue of his housekeeper. Yet Idelette de Bure never complained. Not only was she patient, eager to serve her husband, and glad to share him with whatever of the Lord's work he had to do, she herself went out to visit the sick, to comfort the sad, and to share her faith with others.

Calvin, warmed by her love, was happier than he had believed possible. Bucer had been right about marriage—it was good to have a wife, a good wife. Even Farel had recommended it—and Farel, past fifty, was still a bachelor!

One cloud hung over the marriage—sickness and poor health. "As if it had been so ordered . . . that our wedlock might not be over joyous, the Lord thus thwarted our joy by moderating it," wrote Calvin to Farel. Less than a month after the wedding, the Calvins had their first of many illnesses.

At the same time there was a tiff with the housekeeper. On a certain Monday the housekeeper spoke rudely, "as oft she does," to brother Antoine, who "silently left the house and vowed solemnly that he would not return so long as she remained with me." Then the housekeeper herself walked out "when she saw me so sad on account of my brother's departure." But her son stayed in the house. For supper on Monday Calvin ate too much. "I am wont . . . when heated by anger, or stirred by some greater anxiety than usual, to eat to excess, . . . which so happened to me at that time." Tuesday he was "tormented in the morning with severe indigestion." Usually at such times he ate nothing. But this time he felt that the son of the housekeeper would "interpret this abstinence to be an indirect way of getting rid of him." So he ate at the table as usual, much to his discomfort, in order not to offend the young man.

Tuesday afternoon he preached with difficulty. At night he fainted. Then came the chills and fevers of tertian fever, bringing severe attacks every other day, after which "I could scarcely lift a finger." And, "while I was still suffering under the weakness . . . my wife took a fever of a different sort. The last eight days she has been so exhausted . . . that she can with difficulty sit up in bed."

Two sick people—through nine years of marriage they carried the burden of frequent illness without complaining. It was enough of happiness to be content, content with each other, and content with whatever God would choose to send into their life together.

23

The Lord's work could not wait for good health. Even during the fever Calvin had been "deliberating with Capito and Bucer, as though I had been quite stout and well."

Important things were afoot. Emperor Charles of Spain, head of the large Holy Roman Empire, was talking about union between the Protestant churches and the Church of Rome. He needed that union, if he could get it, because the fierce armies of the Turks were pushing against his empire from the east. With such trouble marching upon him, the emperor would be better armed if he could unite in religion the German Protestant states with the Roman Catholic ones so that they would fight side by side for the empire.

Emperor Charles decided to arrange some conferences. Imperial diets they were called, and four of them were held in the years 1539 to 1541. The German states and free cities sent delegates to the diets. The prince of each state was there, since he was official head of the church in his area. There were long debates and negotiations. Representatives of the pope and speakers for Protestantism clashed day after day.

Calvin, citizen of Strasbourg, was asked to be one of the delegates from this free German city. At the diets he took no leading part. He was, after all, a Frenchman among Germans, and it was an honor that his German city had sent him. Besides, he had little hope for the success of the diets. How could the Church of Rome and Protestantism go hand in hand? "For my own part, I expect little from it," he wrote to a friend.

But with his eagle eye Calvin watched all that went on. He carefully analyzed each leading person, each important debate. His long letters to Farel were full of details. He was like a reporter covering the world scene of his day. The whole world was discussed at the diets, if not in the main debates, then in all the side talks and conferences.

At the diets Calvin met the German princes and theologians. Chief among these was Philip Melanchthon, Luther's right-hand man, whom Calvin met at Frankfurt in the spring of 1539. A fast friendship sprang up between the two men and lasted twenty-four years until Melanchthon's death. Melanchthon, twelve years older than Calvin, was a man of great learning, accomplished in languages and scholarship. At twenty-one he had been appointed professor of Greek at Wittenberg University. Melanchthon was gentle and peace-loving. Sometimes he was too peace-loving, and he leaned toward compromising on matters where he should have stood more firm. All of his character was in contrast to that of his master, Luther.

Philip Melanchthon must have thought to himself when he met John Calvin, 'So this is the young man who knows the ancient church fathers better than anyone else in the world! What a mind lies behind those piercing eyes!' Melanchthon gave his new French friend a nickname at one of the diets. Calvin had roundly defeated in debate a noted Roman Catholic theologian. From then on Melanchthon spoke of him to others as "The Theologian." Coming from Melanchthon, the name was a real compliment.

As for Calvin, he called Melanchthon a man "of . . . incomparable knowledge, . . . piety, and other virtues," a man "worthy of the admiration of all ages." And later he wrote, "I know that I am far below you." For all of this, Calvin called his friend by first name. He was not slow to tell Philip when it seemed that the German was too quick to compromise, too unwilling to do anything about the many ceremonies or the lax discipline in the German churches. "Of late I have plainly told Philip to his face . . . ," he wrote Farel.

On the one hand, Calvin stood like a rock for what he believed the Bible taught. On the other hand, he never stopped working to draw the Protestant churches together. He was willing to overlook the manmade differences in the churches as long as these differences did not concern basic doctrines. Talking about Bucer, he wrote to Farel, "He cannot endure that on account of these trifling observances we should be separated from Luther. Neither, certainly, do I consider them to be just causes of dissent."

On matters of doctrine as taught in the Word, Calvin did not compromise. He did, however, spend much time working to bring others to believe as he did. "I had much conversation with Philip about many things," said Calvin of his days in Frankfurt, "having written to him beforehand on the subject of agreement."

One of the big subjects the Frenchman and the German discussed was the Lord's Supper. How is the body of Christ present in the Lord's Supper? No, the bread does not become or turn into the body, as the followers of Rome claim. On that Calvin and Melanchthon could agree quickly. But is the body of Christ *with* the bread, in-under-and-above it, as Luther insisted? No, said Calvin, using Scripture, the body and blood of Christ are not physically with the bread and wine. The body and blood of Christ are *spiritually* present.

After the talks at Frankfurt, Calvin happily wrote Farel about Melanchthon, "As for himself, you need not doubt about him, but consider that he is entirely of the same opinion as ourselves." Was this a little beginning of agreement between the Lutherans and Calvin? Having won over the mild Melanchthon, could Melanchthon's master and the German princes be won, too?

On the other side of the Protestant group were the followers of Zwingli, the Swiss reformer. The Zwinglians, too, had convictions about the body of the Lord in the Holy Supper. Following their slain leader, they held that the Supper was only a kind of memorial to the death of Christ. They attached less meaning to it than Calvin did. So Calvin stood in the middle on this matter, between the Lutherans and the Zwinglians. How long did he cherish the hope that he could reach out a hand on either side of him and bring the two groups together?

Calvin had been thinking of this hope when he wrote his *Little Treatise on the Holy Supper of Our Lord.* He wanted it to be the basis for a helpful discussion among Protestant groups. His language in the book was firm, but careful. He did not use the strong words he sometimes put into his writing.

A copy of this little book, translated from French into Latin, was picked up by Martin Luther in 1545 in a bookstore in Germany. Having read it, he said, "I might have entrusted the whole affair of this controversy to him [Calvin] from the beginning. If my opponents had done the like, we should soon have been reconciled."

Martin Luther never met John Calvin. He wrote of him to Bucer, who was Luther's friend. "Salute for me reverently Sturm and Calvin, whose books I have read with special delight," said the great German reformer. Luther had said more about Calvin. Melanchthon reported it to Calvin, and Calvin wrote it to Farel: "Philip . . . wrote thus, 'Luther and Pomeranus have desired Calvin to be greeted; Calvin has acquired favor in their eyes.'" Calvin further reports to Farel, "Philip has informed me that certain persons, in order to irritate Luther, have shown him a passage in which he and his friends have been criticized by me; that thereupon he had examined the passage, and . . . had said at length, 'I hope that Calvin will one day think better of us; but in any event it is well that he should even now have a proof of our good feeling towards him.' If we are not affected by such moderation," adds Calvin, "we are certainly of stone. For myself, I am profoundly affected by it."

A few years later, when Luther began "to thunder most vehemently on the Lord's Supper," Calvin defended him to the leader of the Zwinglians. "Remember what a great man Luther is," he wrote, and enumerated his accomplishments. "Even if he would call me a devil," ended Calvin, "I would yet honor him and call him an illustrious servant of God."

Calvin wrote a letter to Luther, too, in the years before Luther's death when the German was more peevish and quick to anger than before. Calvin sent the letter to Melanchthon, who never passed it on to his master. "I have not shown your letter to Dr. Martin," Melanchthon explained to Calvin. "He takes up many things suspiciously, and does not like his replies to questions of the kind you have proposed to him, to be carried round and handed from one to another." In Calvin's undelivered letter, he had sent a few of his writings, asking for the comments of Luther, and had ended, "Would that I might fly to you, that I might even for a few hours enjoy the happiness of your company. . . . But seeing this is not granted to us on earth, I hope that it will shortly come to pass in the kingdom of God. Farewell, most renowned sir, most distinguished minister of Christ, and my ever-honored father."

Who can say what might have happened to the Protestant church if the Lord had chosen to bring the

Reformation giants to believe the same basic truths from the Word? If that day was ever near, it was near when such men as Calvin, Luther, and Melanchthon knew each other in person or by letter. Though they never reached the agreement and the unity of which Calvin dreamed, they spoke of each other in words of friendship and esteem. Despite their differences, they considered each other brothers in Christ.

We today might learn that lesson from the great reformers.

24

John Calvin was weeping. He choked the sobs in his throat to stifle the sound of them. He covered his face with his hands.

Beside the weeping man lay a letter. Several men had traveled hundreds of miles on horseback to deliver it. They had gone first to Strasbourg, expecting to find the French preacher there. Pastor Calvin is in Worms, the Strasbourg city council had told the messengers. He is representing our city at the third imperial diet there.

The messengers had ridden on and entered the city gate of Worms. Urging their horses through the crowded streets, they had inquired until they found the man to whom their letter was addressed. Gravely they had delivered it to him.

To Doctor Calvin, Minister of the Gospel—these were the words of formal address on the outside of the letter. Inside, in warmer tone, it continued:

> Monsieur, our Good Brother and Special Friend: We commend ourselves very affectionately to you, for that we are thoroughly informed that you have no other desire than the growth and advancement of the glory and honor of God, and of His sacred and holy Word. On the part of Little, Great, and General Councils, . . . we pray you very earnestly that you would transfer yourself hitherward to us, and return to your old place and former ministry; and we hope, with the help of God, that this shall be a great benefit, and fruitful for the increase of the holy Evangel, seeing that our people greatly desire you among us, and will conduct themselves toward you in such sort, that you shall have occasion to rest content.
>
> Your good friends,
> The Syndics and Council of Geneva
> October 22, 1540

The official seal of the city was in wax at the bottom. On it was the motto, *Post Tenebras Spero Lucem*—"After Darkness I Hope for Light."

And now the man so urgently invited to return to Geneva sat with the letter, weeping. The messengers were gone, having added their own words of entreaty to the message of the letter. Around Calvin sat the Strasbourg men who were with him in Worms for the imperial diet. He had called them to ask their advice. Twice as he talked with them, Calvin left the room to control the tears that interrupted his words.

Help me, Calvin begged his companions. Tell me what I must do. Do not consider me and my feelings.

Think only of what is best for the growth of the Gospel and the glory of God. I am in a daily agony. You know I have been struggling with this decision and I know not what to answer. Help me, my trusted friends. I lean on you.

The men of Strasbourg answered earnestly. Good brother, they said, you know how our city wishes to keep you. When the messengers of Geneva came to Strasbourg, the council of Strasbourg sent a swift horseman to us here in Worms to tell us to keep you from promising Geneva anything. When we consider what to us seems most for the glory of Christ, we long to keep you in Strasbourg. But if the will of God is otherwise, how can we stand in your way? Yet, wait until the diet has ended, and then consider what the Lord would have you do.

Calvin waited in the same city where almost twenty years earlier Martin Luther had taken his brave stand before the emperor. "Here I stand. I cannot do otherwise. So help me God." These had been Luther's immortal words. And now Calvin was in the same walled city, far from home and his new wife, crowded with many other delegates into the large common sleeping-room of an inn. He was still weak from the tertian fever which had attacked him in September. Waiting, he spent time with Melanchthon. He debated privately on matters of faith. Here in Worms he earned Melanchthon's nickname, "The Theologian."

Daily the hundreds of delegates grew more restless. There was no sign that the diet would begin. The Duke of Granvelle, appointed to head the diet, had not yet arrived. Finally, almost a month late, he appeared in Worms. Then came weeks of discussion to set up the order and method of the debate. At last, on January 14, 1541, the actual debate began. Calvin had been in Worms since November 1 of the preceding year!

In that two and a half months he went on wrestling with the problem of Geneva. It was not a new problem. The letter delivered in Worms had been no surprise. It was only an added weight to the burden already pressing on him. The burden of Geneva—had he ever been free of it, even when he left the rebellious city, even when he became a citizen of peaceful Strasbourg?

Five months after leaving Geneva, Calvin had written a letter to the church there. Nine months later he had written again, counseling the members to peace and brotherly love. In September 1539 he had spent six days writing fifteen thousand words of reply to the cardinal who was trying to persuade Geneva to return to the Church of Rome. What a reply that had been! The cardinal had not ventured to open his eloquent mouth again.

This learned cardinal, Sadolet, had written a flattering, persuasive letter to Geneva in April of 1539. In it he praised the city and its people in extravagant language. How sad that rabble-rousing Protestants should have created a disturbance in your faithful Roman Catholic church, said Sadolet. Now that you Genevans have triumphantly put these troublesome ministers out of your city, may we lovingly invite you to return to the arms of the mother church, the eternal Church of Rome?

No one in Geneva had been able to answer the impressive letter of Sadolet. Friends of Calvin sent him a copy and suggested he reply. How could he refuse? Not only to save Geneva from falling back to

Rome, but because he was still a part of Geneva, he answered the cardinal. Writing of the church of Geneva, Calvin told Sadolet, "God, when He charged me with it, bound me to be faithful to it forever. So, now, when I see the worst snares laid for that church, whose safety it has pleased the Lord to make my highest care, . . . who will advise me to await the issue silent and unconcerned?" In that conviction Calvin wrote his fifteen thousand words to the cardinal. Sadolet was silenced.

In Strasbourg Calvin continued to hear news of what was happening in Geneva. The four new ministers of the Geneva church were weak men, willing to follow the crowd. Two of them were stooges for Bern. The wild living in the city grew wilder. People even went parading naked down the streets to the tune of fife and drum.

Slowly the reaction set in. The councils passed more severe laws, even though they did not enforce them. The four syndics who had opposed Calvin were out of power. One was hanged for treason against the city. He was guilty of plotting to turn Geneva over to Bern. Another syndic, accused of the same crime, jumped out of the window of a house on the city wall and broke his neck that way instead of in the noose. The other two syndics hastily escaped from the city. Then the two ministers who had been sent by Bern left, too.

In all the uproar the feeling grew that Geneva could not survive without the firm hand of Master Calvin. As early as March of 1540, less than a year after Calvin's expulsion, friends wrote him that they hoped he would be asked to return. Shuddering, Calvin wrote Farel, "Rather would I submit to death a hundred times than to that cross, on which one had to perish daily a thousand times over. This . . . information I . . . communicate to you, that to the utmost of your power you may . . . oppose the measures of those who shall endeavor to draw me back thither."

The lovable Peter Viret, pastor in Lausanne, had heard the rumor, too. He had written Calvin, encouraging him to consider Geneva, also because of its mountain air and good climate. With a wry smile, Calvin answered in May of 1540, "I read that passage of your letter, certainly not without a smile, where you show so much concern about my health, and recommend Geneva on that ground. . . . It would have been far preferable to perish once for all than to be tormented again in that place of torture. Therefore, my dear Viret, if you wish me well, make no mention of such a proposal."

In the autumn of 1540 the councils of Geneva took action. On September 21 the Little Council asked one of its leading members, Ami Perrin, "to find means, if he could, to bring back Master Calvin." On October 13 it was decided to write a letter "to Monsieur Calvin that he would assist us." On October 19 the Council of Two Hundred resolved "in order that the honor and glory of God may be promoted" to secure "Master Calvin as preacher." And on October 20 the people of Geneva gathered as the General Council. "We must have Calvin," they shouted, and wholeheartedly decided "to send to Strasbourg to fetch Master John Calvin, who is very learned, to be minister in this city."

And so the letters and the special messengers began to reach Calvin. Geneva also asked the Protestant cantons of Bern and Zurich to persuade Strasbourg to relinquish its outstanding citizen. Zurich was willing, but Bern was rather cool about the whole business, being unable to assume any authority over Geneva, as it wished to do.

Many people wrote their private letters of urging. "Triumph, come quickly, brother, come, come, that we may rejoice in God our Redeemer," wrote one. Another, one of the ministers who had left the city, wrote, "Do not say 'No.' You would resist the Holy Spirit, not men. Remember the fruits waiting to be harvested in France. The Genevan church is important . . . no mortal man is able to direct it with such force, so wisely and so ably as you." One of the two remaining ministers who had formerly spoken against Calvin, now said, "Come, honored father in Christ, you belong to us, the Lord Himself has given you to us. Everyone sighs for you."

Viret, who had consented to go to Geneva for six months as a temporary helper, wrote his friend, "Do not linger, come to build up and to gladden the church which lies in misery, grief, and sorrow."

And Farel—as often as he could find a messenger, he would send a bombshell of a letter to the man he had once ordered to stay in Geneva. Calvin, wrestling with his decision, replied to one of Farel's letters, "The thunderbolts which you so strangely hurl at me, for what reasons I know not, have filled me with the greatest terror and dismay. You know that I have dreaded this summons, but that I have not been deaf to it. Then why attack me with such violence as almost to disrupt our friendship?"

To the Magnificent and Honorable Lords Messieurs the Syndics and Council of Geneva, Calvin had written with gracious courtesy from Strasbourg on October 23, 1540, ". . . I can testify before God that I hold your church in such consideration that I would never be wanting in her time of need to do whatsoever I could for her help. . . . On the other hand, I cannot slightingly quit the charge . . . to which the Lord has called me [in Strasbourg], without being relieved of it by regular and faithful means. . . . Moreover, it has been arranged by . . . the council of . . . Strasbourg that I should go with some of my brethren to the Assembly at Worms, not to serve one church solely, but for the common interest, in which number yours is included. . . . I promise you that nothing shall be denied you on my part in all that is allowable, but that I will do my uttermost to serve you so far as God permits."

From Worms Calvin again wrote the honorable lords of Geneva after their latest delegation of messengers had reached him. It may be necessary for me to attend another imperial diet, he told the councilmen, but "the instant . . . I shall be freed from this extraordinary employment" I promise you I will do what I can to help you, if the church and council of Strasbourg will free me.

To Farel Calvin wrote in October of 1540, "When I consider that I am not in my own power, I offer my heart a slain victim for a sacrifice to the Lord. . . . I yield my soul chained and bound unto obedience to God." This was the only way. It was the only way, even if it led back to Geneva, the city of which Calvin had written Viret, "There is no place under heaven of which I can have a greater dread."

But the human side of Calvin struggled against going back to the city on the lake. It would be "to perish daily a thousand times over." He wrote the Zurich pastors who had sent a letter urging his return to Geneva, "Were I, therefore, to give way to my own feelings, I would rather go beyond the sea than return thither."

As the months passed, the decision became clearer. "Somehow, I cannot tell how it happens, I begin to feel more of an inclination to take the helm in hand," Calvin wrote Viret. The decision was not pleasant. But it was clear. The Strasbourg church had agreed to let him go, though Bucer insisted it would be for only a little while, until things in Geneva were straightened out. Meanwhile, we will keep you as a citizen always and pay you your professor's salary, offered the Strasbourg city council. The citizenship Calvin accepted as a mark of the council's esteem. The salary he declined.

The diet at Worms had failed. After three days of formal debate, the emperor had sent orders to have it adjourned, which was the usual procedure when no progress was in sight. The fourth diet was set for March in the German city of Ratisbon. Calvin and his companions came home from Worms on January 23, 1541. They had been gone from Strasbourg almost three months. After one month at home, they were on the road again, jolting along in a carriage, wrapped in furs and blankets to protect them from the freezing weather.

It was a long trip to Ratisbon, a city in the heart of the Roman Catholic territories. The ice on the Danube River thawed enough to let the Strasbourg men travel seven days on a large raft. Their carriage and horses floated with them the raft, along with their books and papers, cooking equipment, blankets, and clothing. "I am dragged most unwillingly to Ratisbon," wrote Calvin to Farel. "I foresee that the journey will prove very troublesome, . . . I much fear that there may be a prolonged delay, for they are wont, ofttimes, to lengthen out the diets even for ten months. . . . But I shall follow wherever God leads, who knows best why He has laid this necessity upon me."

In Ratisbon Calvin and his companions heard the grim news that the plague was raging in Strasbourg. Everyone who could was fleeing for his life. Idelette had gone to her brother. Brother Antoine and stepsister Marie had escaped to a little town nearby. Claude Ferey, a French refugee and teacher, one of Calvin's dearest friends, was dead. So was a boarder in Calvin's house, a boy of whom he was very fond. In a remarkable letter from Ratisbon, Calvin poured out his sympathy to the father of the dead boy. He wrote Farel, "Day and night my wife is constantly in my thoughts, being as she is alone and comfortless, and without support." Worried and grief-stricken, the Strasbourg men sat in Ratisbon, waiting for the largest of the four diets to begin.

March, April, May, and the debates were inching along. There was some agreement, amazingly, until the matter of the Holy Supper presented the usual stone wall. Calvin continued to write long reports to Farel. "Philip and Bucer have drawn up ambiguous and insincere formulas concerning transubstantiation," he wrote, "to try whether they could satisfy the opposite party by yielding nothing. I cannot agree to this," though both of these good men are proceeding "with the best intentions, and have no other object . . . than promoting the kingdom of Christ."

Nothing can come of this, Calvin told himself and asked Bucer to let him go back to Strasbourg. Bucer agreed reluctantly, and Calvin made the long trip back, arriving June 25.

Except for the joy of seeing Idelette alive, it was a bleak homecoming. In his own home and in the homes of many others were the empty places of those whom the plague had carried away. Calvin made his rounds, comforting the families in grief. He preached to his refugee congregation again. He looked at the familiar people and places in Strasbourg wistfully, as one about to say farewell to all of them. The letters kept coming from Geneva and other parts of Switzerland. He had made his promise before God. Could he wait any longer to return to Geneva?

"Are you waiting for the stones to cry out?" Farel had roared vehemently in his latest letter. "If you had been as slow to leave, when we were ordered out of the city, as you are slow to return despite all pleas, things would not have reached their present pass!"

The councils of Geneva sent an official herald on horseback to wait for Calvin and to escort him back. The council of Strasbourg, willing but reluctant to see their French pastor leave, sent a letter to Geneva. "Finally he comes to you," said the letter, "this incomparable, this rare instrument of the Lord. Our century knows of no other like him—indeed, if besides him one can still speak of another. . . ."

Early in September of 1541, escorted by the herald, Calvin set out for Geneva. He and Idelette had decided wisely that she should stay behind until he sent for her.

Tears clouding his eyes, Calvin rode away from the peaceful city where he had spent three fruitful years. The Lord was sending him back to the storms of Geneva. No one, least of all Calvin, dreamed that in eight years his French refugee church would be forced by the emperor's edict to leave the peaceful city of Strasbourg, and that Bucer would be forced to an exile in England. Nor did anyone, least of all Calvin, dream that the tempestuous city to which he was going would become for all time the Reformation city of the world.

On Tuesday, September 13, 1541, two men on horseback approached the old Cornavin gate of Geneva. Ahead of them soared the towers of Saint Pierre.

The sentry in armor at the gate peered out through his helmet and watched the men approach. The first man on horseback wore the costume of a Genevan herald and carried the flag of the city. But who was the second man, wrapped in a black cloak? The sentry looked again and then he knew.

This was the man for whom the whole city of Geneva was waiting.

Part III
After Darkness Light

25

Geneva had Calvin again.

He was standing in the familiar council chamber in his black robe, with twenty-five faces turned toward him. The men of the Little Council looked at him intently. He was older and more dignified than when they had ordered him out of their city. He seemed more gracious and courteous than they remembered him. They knew he was more famous, too, spoken of all over Europe.

The councilmen were relieved to have Calvin back. Geneva could not get along without him. They had some gifts ready as a welcome. There was a new robe of black velvet, trimmed with fur, and a house on Canon Street, a short, narrow street near the cathedral. At the back of the house was a garden which overlooked the blue lake. In Saint Pierre there was a new pulpit waiting, a graceful, carved, wooden one fastened to one of the massive stone pillars. The councils sent a herald and a two-horse carriage to bring Madame Calvin and her daughter Judith from Strasbourg. And the clerk recorded the decision of the twenty-five councilmen, "Resolved to keep Calvin here always."

Geneva had Calvin back. And Calvin had Geneva back. He had not asked to have it back. He had not asked for it the first time he stopped as a traveler to stay one night. He had not asked for Strasbourg either, for that matter. But he was not his own master. His heart, "a slain sacrifice," was willingly offered to the Lord. He was ready to go wherever his Master sent him. Yet, remembering the ugly mobs and the endless wickedness of Geneva, it was impossible not to shrink back a little. Calvin wrote Farel, with a small note of blame in the words, "As you wished, I am settled here; may the Lord overrule it for good."

Wasting no time, Calvin proposed plans. "Immediately after I had offered my services to the council," he wrote Farel, "I declared that a church could not hold together unless a settled government should be agreed on, such as is prescribed to us in the Word of God, and such as was in use in the ancient church. Then I touched gently upon certain points. . . ."

Firmly but gently—that was the way. Concentrate on the big things. Overlook the little things that irritate and bother. Bear hatred toward no one. Forgive what is past. And, at all costs, do not give way to anger. Do this in spite of headache and stomachache and asthma and any other illness. Do this in spite of every enemy and trouble lying low beneath a smooth surface of welcome. Do it in a city where the church of Christ has fallen into chaos, and where reforming it means reforming the whole city, because the whole city belongs to the church. "God and the angels, who see us" looked down on the burdened man in the house on Canon Street and found him often on his knees, praying, his Bible open before him. He was praying for his own strength as well as for the church and the city to which he had been called.

A day or two after Calvin's return, the great Clemence bell of Saint Pierre called the people for a special service. The councils attended in a body, their members dressed in the black and gray colors of the city. Calvin stood in the new pulpit, speaking solemnly about the awful events in the world. The Turks were overrunning Hungary. The plague raged in the cities and villages of Germany. In France the fires of fierce persecution were burning. Let us humble ourselves before the Lord, said the clear voice from the new pulpit. Let us pray for the world and for our brethren. And may the Lord God Almighty take our city under His protection. Amen.

On the first Sunday John Calvin was in the pulpit again. The people waited for him to speak about the reasons for his exile and return. But he spoke no word of blame. It was his custom to preach through a book of the Bible, chapter by chapter, verse by verse. He began to preach at the exact verse where he had discontinued three years before.

"For the first month after resuming the ministry, I had so much to attend to and so many annoyances, that I was almost worn out. . . . This, however, somewhat consoles and refreshes me, that we do not

139

labor altogether in vain, without some fruit appearing." This was Calvin writing to a friend in Basel. He was keeping Viret in Geneva to help him, telling Farel, "I shall not suffer [him] on any account to be dragged away from me."

To Bucer, the fatherly pastor left behind in Strasbourg, Calvin wrote humbly, a month after returning to Geneva, "Insofar as depends on me, I shall give ground of offense to no one. . . . Until . . . I can bear no more, you need not question my faithful performance of what I have promised you. And if in any way I do not answer your expectation, you know that I am under your power, and subject to your authority. Admonish, chastise, and exercise all the powers of a father over his son. Pardon my haste. . . . I am entangled in so many employments, that I am almost beside myself."

Meanwhile, Idelette was unpacking and settling down in the house at Number 11 Canon Street. It was a welcome change from the boardinghouse in Strasbourg. The councils had put some furniture in the house. It was the sort of stuff they loaned to any minister of Geneva. There were two walnut bedsteads and one of maple for the three little bedrooms upstairs. For the downstairs rooms, a living room, study, and kitchen, there were such pieces as a square walnut table with maple bench, a walnut sideboard, two walnut trunks bound in iron, four long tables of pine wood, two more walnut tables, a dozen wooden chairs or stools, and a desk. The desk went into the study, along with two benches, one for Calvin and one for visitors. In the study there were also a tall bookcase and a little set of portable, wooden steps for reaching books on the top shelves. Idelette made the house more attractive with the things she had brought from Strasbourg.

At the head of the short, narrow street was a water fountain where women washed clothes and drew water for their homes. Here the horses also stopped to quench their thirst.

In the garden at the back of her house, Idelette grew vegetables. She could manage tolerably well on her husband's salary from Geneva. Calvin was paid five hundred florins a year, and in addition, twelve measures of corn and two casks of wine. This was enough flour to bake about twelve hundred loaves of bread, more than twenty a week. It was enough wine for a couple of bottles a day. Calvin's salary was a little higher than that paid the other ministers, because, said the councils, Master Calvin will be entertaining many people who pass through the city. Sometimes the people did not only pass through. They stayed in the small house on Canon Street, and Idelette was hard pressed to stretch her bread and wine.

Calvin's stepsister Marie married a Genevan named Costan and lived in a house of her own. His brother Antoine was married the year after Calvin's return to Geneva. After a while Antoine purchased a country villa outside the city walls, but he and his family usually lived in the house on Canon Street.

Calvin, Idelette, Idelette's daughter Judith, Antoine, his wife Ann, their four small children—all of these lived in the Calvin house. Besides, there was the steady stream of visitors and messengers passing in and out of the door.

Not in a quiet retreat, but in the middle of this hubbub of activity, Calvin prepared sermons and lectures, wrote letters, and set down in longhand his great books and writings.

26

Calvin began his second stay in Geneva by writing a document. The Little Council had agreed to a "settled government" for the church, and only two weeks after his return, Calvin had the detailed report ready. The *Ecclesiastical Ordinances of the Church of Geneva* was submitted for approval to the councils of the city. In the document were many of the ideas that had grown and matured in Calvin's mind during his peaceful years in Strasbourg.

The Little Council debated and made some changes in the *Ordinances*. The Council of Two Hundred did the same. Both councils made sure that their power over the church was firmly stated. They needed Calvin back in Geneva, but they had no intention of letting him or the church take over any of their authority. Without showing the revised copy to the ministers, the councils called the citizens together. Under Saint Pierre's high-vaulted roof, the people, meeting as the General Council, approved the *Ordinances* on Sunday, November 20, 1541.

The *Ordinances* spoke of many things.

They began by setting up four offices in the church—minister, teacher, elder, and deacon. This was the heart of Calvin's plan for the church of Geneva. He patterned it after the New Testament church. Carefully he set forth the specifications and duties of each sacred office.

There was also a full program for the church. "Each Sunday there is to be a sermon at Saint Pierre and Saint Gervais at break of day, and at the usual hour [nine o'clock]. . . . At midday, there is to be catechism, that is, instruction of little children in all the three churches. . . . At three o'clock second sermon. . . . Besides . . . , on working days there will be a sermon at Saint Pierre three times a week, on Monday, Wednesday, and Friday." The people of Geneva would have ample chance to hear the Word of God if they went to church faithfully.

Baptism was to take place in church, not at home, with the font near the pulpit, not near the door. For the Lord's Supper "the tables should be beside the pulpit," and the people should come forward in groups to take their places at the tables.

"No one is to be totally confined to bed for three days without informing the minister. . . ." "Saturday after dinner" is the time set for visiting prisoners, including "anyone in irons, whom it is not desirable to take out." And so on.

The thorny problem of who had power to excommunicate—Calvin tackled that again, too, though more tactfully. For certain persistent sins, after three warnings, a man must be informed by the church to "abstain from the Supper until a change of life is seen." But, even in the rebellious city of Geneva, this "should be done with . . . moderation, . . . for even the corrections are only medicines for bringing back sinners to our Lord." Was this harsh?

143

Calvin wrote the *Ordinances* for the church of Geneva. But churches all over the world have made use of this famous document. It is the foundation of church government in all the Reformed and Presbyterian churches, though they have made some changes in it to fit their own time and place. For example, Calvin had to agree, "in the present condition of the church," to have the elders appointed by the city councils, because in his time and city the church and government were tied together. This was not what Calvin wanted. In his *Institutes* he had made clear the need for a church free from government control. But the most important thing was that Calvin reestablished the church offices of elder and deacon, following the New Testament pattern. There were no lay elders and deacons in the Church of Rome. Calvin restored the layman to a place of authority and leadership in the church of Christ.

The *Ordinances,* argued and revised in the councils, still kept the basic ideas of Calvin, which were to influence churches in many lands and centuries. In place of a title on the document, the councils wrote these words.

"In the Name of Almighty God, we, the Syndics of the Little and the Great Councils with our people assembled at the sound of trumpet and great bell, according to our ancient customs, . . . have commanded and established to be followed and observed in our city and territory the Ecclesiastical Constitution which follows, seeing that it is taken from the Gospel of Jesus Christ."

To have the *Ordinances* accepted on paper was one accomplishment. To put the document into practice in the lives of the people was another. It took

144

two months to pass the paper *Ordinances*. It took fourteen stormy years to put them into practice.

Before the first rumblings of discontent were heard, terror struck Geneva.

"The plague creeps toward us," wrote Calvin to Bucer. "If it has spared us for this winter, we shall scarcely escape in the spring."

27

The streets of Geneva were deserted. Schools and shops were closed. Those few people who came to church on Sundays sat far apart, eyeing each other suspiciously. The only sound to be heard in the empty streets was the jangling of the bells on the death wagon. Into it were piled the bodies of the dead, who could not have a decent burial because their bodies carried the dread germs. Outside the city walls, the hospital called the pesthouse was crowded with sick and dying.

The plague had come to Geneva. It was spring 1542. Some said that Swiss soldiers passing through the city had brought the deadly epidemic. In the narrow streets, with lack of sanitation, it spread like wildfire.

What pastor would go to the bedside of the plague-stricken to comfort them and prepare their hearts for dying? The French refugee, Pastor Peter

Blanchet, stepped forward. "His offer is accepted," read the council record. He entered the plague hospital outside the walls and went faithfully from cot to cot until he himself lay sick, dying, dead.

Calvin had offered himself, despite his own poor health and his concern for Idelette, who was expecting their first child. The council records say that Calvin at that time was refused in his offer to serve in the plague hospital, "on account of the great need which the church has of his services."

The plague was raging in many cities. It attacked Strasbourg, too. There Bucer lost his gracious wife Elizabeth, who for twenty years had cared for him and for all the refugees who found shelter in Bucer's home. Four of the six Bucer children also died. And Capito, the comrade minister of Bucer, the learned senior pastor, was killed by the plague. He was buried the day before Elizabeth Bucer died.

In Geneva the plague came and went. It was back again in 1545. Another young minister volunteered to serve in the plague hospital, and died there. The people, hysterical with fear, believed that a horrible scheme was at work. They thought that some men and women, in league with attendants of the plague hospital, were making an ointment containing infected matter from the patients. This stuff they smeared on door latches in the city, spreading the plague in the hope that they could get the possessions of the people who died. Calvin, too, believed that this was happening. Perhaps it was. To a friend in Basel Calvin wrote, "The Lord is sorely trying us in this quarter. A conspiracy of men and women has lately been discovered, who, for the space of three years, have spread the plague through the city. . . . Fifteen

146

women have been burnt; some men have been punished even more severely; some have committed suicide in prison; and while twenty-five are still kept prisoners, the conspirators do not cease, notwithstanding, to smear the doorlocks of the dwelling houses with their poisonous ointment. You see in the midst of what perils we are tossed about. The Lord has hitherto preserved our house, though it has more than once been attempted."

While the Lord preserved the house on Canon Street from the plague, He had sent a deep sorrow into it. In late July of 1542, Calvin wrote his friend Viret, who had just returned to his church in Lausanne, "In what great anxiety I am at present writing to you! My wife has been delivered prematurely, not without danger; may the Lord have a care over us."

Calvin baptized his little son Jacques. The child lingered two weeks and then died. Idelette did not recover strength quickly. In August, writing Viret again, Calvin said, "Greet . . . your wife, to whom mine returns her thanks for so much friendly and pious consolation. She is unable to reply, except by a secretary, and it would be very difficult for her even to dictate a letter. The Lord has certainly inflicted a severe and bitter wound in the death of our infant son. But He is Himself a father, and knows what is good for His children."

Almost twenty years later, the pastor of Geneva replied to an enemy's accusation: "Balduin twits me . . . that I have no children," answered Calvin. "God had given me a son. God has taken my little boy. . . . But I have myriads of sons throughout the Christian world." These would be Calvin's sons, his spiritual sons, following his teaching and example.

Three years after the little Jacques died, a daughter was born. She, too, died. Once more, two years later, Calvin wrote a friend about the baptism of the third child the Calvins were expecting. But the baptism never took place. The baby died at birth. And Idelette, in continued poor health, went slowly about her work in the house and the garden. Besides her weakness, it was her coughing, the endless coughing, that dragged her down.

Despite poor health, it was Idelette who brought peacefulness and order to the house on Canon Street. When she was well, she herself received the stream of visitors that knocked at the door. Many she fed and lodged. Even when she was sick, the Calvin home was open to guests. "Your hospitality in the name of Christ is not unknown to anybody in Europe," someone wrote Calvin two years before Idelette died.

No one knows how often the quiet sympathy and loving care of Idelette brought peace to the busy, intense man who was her husband. Calvin worked in a way that would have exhausted any healthy man. At five in the morning he was up and busy. If he was ill, he was in bed and busy, with books spread out on his coverlet. On Sundays he preached two or three times in Saint Pierre. During alternate weeks he preached the weekday sermons on Monday, Wednesday, and Friday. Every week he gave public lectures on Tuesday, Thursday, and Saturday. On Thursdays he also presided over the consistory meetings, at which all the ministers and elders met to study the Scriptures. Calvin took his part in visiting the sick and the prisoners. He regularly visited the families of his parish, as he had said in the *Ordinances* that it should be done.

These were the regular duties. But they were only a beginning. Calvin was always writing letters. To his door galloped couriers from all over Europe, delivering letters and waiting to carry away their answers. Anyone in the city who wanted to send or receive a letter could arrange to do it on Canon Street. The Calvin house was Geneva's post office.

Besides letters of advice and help, Calvin was writing pamphlets, tracts, treatises, and books. He was editing his commentaries, which were his public lectures recorded by secretaries. He lectured on one book of the Bible after another, treating each chapter and verse in detail.

The councils of Geneva made good use of the man they had asked to return. At their request, Calvin edited and compiled the laws of the city. With the secretary of the Little Council, Claude Roset, Calvin worked hour after hour untangling the confusion of the law books. He was classifying the laws now. Later he would ask for changes in them.

Could a man have been busier? There was still more to do. Marriages and baptisms had to be performed and then registered at the town hall in Calvin's small, angular handwriting. Or some needy creature stood at his door, like the man whom Calvin sent on to the city hospital with this note to the man in charge, "This poor man is so disfigured, that it is pitiful. . . . Will you consider whether you can manage to help him? . . . He must belong to the town, for had he been a stranger, I would myself have provided for him in some way."

Worst of all, Calvin had enemies to fight. It was nothing new to be attacked by men and groups within Geneva, or by men from other places, who disagreed with Calvin's doctrines. But every battle was a struggle. The man who longed for peace and privacy would need to cast aside his natural shyness and reluctance. He would need to be bold and fearless in defending what he believed from Scripture. Sometimes, pushing himself to battle, he would be too forceful in the words he used or the punishments he recommended.

Yet in the early years of his return to Geneva, Calvin held his anger firmly in check. Perhaps Idelette deserved some of the credit for this. Inconspicuous in Geneva, unknown in history, she was content to stay in the background, patient, quiet, serving the famous man she had married.

28

"Death is come up into our windows, and is entered into our palaces," said the Old Testament prophet Jeremiah in his day. His words were also true of the five years from 1544 to 1549.

In 1546, in the palace of England, died Henry VIII, the king of many wives. He left his throne to the boy king, Edward VI, ten-year-old son of his third wife, Jane Seymour. The next year death struck in the palace of France. Fickle King Francis I gave up the earthly crown he had worn for thirty-two years. The years of his reign had been filled with the hangings, beheadings, and burnings of many Protestants. His son, Henry II, began to persecute more fiercely than his father had done.

Two years after Francis I died, Margaret, queen of Navarre and the king's sister, died in Paris. She had loved her brother Francis deeply. But she had also befriended and sheltered many a man whom her brother would have allowed the Church of Rome to persecute and kill.

Clement Marot was no king, but he left the world a treasure when he died in 1544 in Turin, Italy. This French poet had translated some of the psalms into poetry. The first psalms he prepared were sung to popular tunes and became great favorites, especially in France. King Francis liked to sing when he went hunting, "As pants the hart for streams of living water." Calvin used Marot's psalms, set to new tunes, in his Strasbourg and Geneva psalmbooks. He had first met the French poet in 1536 at the court of Ferrara, to which Marot had fled from Paris. In 1543 Marot spent some months in Geneva, and Calvin persuaded the councils to hire him to translate fifty more psalms. These were used in the famous *Genevan Psalter* of 1562. From Geneva, Marot went on to Turin where he died.

Popes also lived in palaces. Though they claimed to speak and act for God, they had no power over death. In 1549, the reigning pope, Paul III, died. He would be remembered as the pope who excommunicated King Henry VIII from the Church of Rome, who approved Loyola's Order of Jesuits, and who appointed the great Michelangelo to be chief architect of the Vatican and of Saint Peter's Cathedral in Rome. Pope Paul's body lay in state, and his feet, extended through an iron railing, were kissed by the faithful throngs who came to pay their last respects.

Of all the deaths in these five years, the death of Martin Luther brought the most sorrow to Protestants. In January of 1546 Luther had gone from his Wittenberg home to Eisleben, the village of his birth. He had made the cold trip in a covered cart. On a Sunday he preached in the church where he had been baptized. Suddenly, the night before he was to travel home, he became ill and died.

Martin Luther, sixty-two years old, was buried with solemn pomp and ceremony in the Castle Church of Wittenberg, on whose door he had nailed his ninety-five theses. Nearby, also buried beneath the stone floor, lay the body of Prince Frederick, Luther's protector. Melanchthon stood at the burial, weeping. He wept for the death of his master. He wept also for the troubles and disagreements that had entered the Lutheran states in the last years of Luther's life. There would be more of that bitter disagreement. It would break out afresh now that Luther had died. In Germany there would be no strong leader to succeed the man who was called the father of the Reformation.

The strong leader would be found elsewhere—in the house on Canon Street in Geneva. What Luther with his heroic courage had begun, Calvin would continue and complete with a brilliant mind and a pen never at rest. Luther had wrenched the Protestant church out of the Church of Rome. He had brought the Reformation. Calvin would establish and apply it. He would put the Reformation truths on paper and explain how the rediscovered Word of God reaches into every part of life.

The reformer of Geneva did not realize this as he sat at his desk or made his familiar way over the cobblestones to Saint Pierre and the town hall. He was in the middle of many battles when Martin Luther died. He was preaching and lecturing. He was receiving visitors and writing letters. He was writing books and treatises. Sick or well, he moved through every day without flinching.

No one saw in the piercing eyes and the firmly-set mouth that a new sorrow was gnawing at Calvin's heart. Idelette was sick. Textor, the doctor, was often at her bedside, but this time he could not help her. In August of 1548 Calvin wrote Viret, "My wife commends herself to your prayers. She is so overpowered with her sickness that she can scarcely support herself. Frequently she seems somewhat better, but she soon relapses." The weakness and the spells of coughing—were they signs of tuberculosis, a disease unknown to doctors of that day?

In early March of 1549 Idelette became too weak to be helped from her bed. Her husband was embroiled in endless duties and problems. Refugees were pouring into the crowded city from France and even from Italy. They needed housing and work. The Libertines, the lovers of loose living, did all they could to irritate Calvin and to stir up the city against him. He was editing the commentary on Hebrews, dedicated to Sigismund Augustus, king of Poland. In the endless round of duties he searched for time to spend in the sickroom until the next duty tore him away again.

Idelette was peacefully waiting to die. She had not complained during her lifetime, and she was not complaining now. Three days before her death a group gathered in her room to pray with her. One of the ministers "in the name of the rest, exhorted her to faith and patience. She briefly (for she was now greatly worn) testified to what was in her heart." Calvin reassured her that he would care for her children, the young man in Strasbourg and the girl Judith in the house on Canon Street. Idelette answered in a whisper, "I have already committed them to the Lord." Calvin replied that this would not prevent him from doing what he could for them, and she answered haltingly, "I know that you will not neglect those whom you know to be committed to the Lord."

On March 29, the day of her death, Idelette listened carefully to the words of a minister who had come to comfort her. She "spoke aloud, so that all saw that her heart was raised far above the world. For these were her words, 'O glorious resurrection. O God of Abraham, and of all our fathers, in Thee have the faithful trusted during so many past ages, and none of them have trusted in vain. I too will hope.' These sentences were rather ejaculated than distinctly spoken. I had to go out at six o'clock"—this is Calvin pouring out the details to Farel in a letter. "Having been moved to another room after seven, she immediately began to decline. When she felt her voice suddenly failing her, she said, 'Let us pray; let us pray. All pray for me.' I had now returned. She was unable to speak, and her mind seemed to be troubled. I, having spoken a few words about the love of Christ, the hope of eternal life, about our married life together, and her departure, engaged in prayer. . . . She both heard the prayer, and attended to it. Before eight she died, so calmly, that those present could scarcely distinguish between her life and her death."

The burdened man in the house on Canon Street was alone. "Truly mine is no ordinary . . . grief," he wrote Viret a week later. "I have been bereaved of the best companion of my life." And to Farel, "I do what I can to keep myself from being overwhelmed with grief. My friends also leave nothing undone that may bring relief to my mental suffering. . . . May the Lord Jesus . . . support me . . . under this heavy affliction, which would certainly have overcome me, had not He, who raises up the prostrate, strengthens the weak, and refreshes the weary, stretched forth His hand from heaven to me."

In the last weeks of Idelette's life, Calvin had not missed a sermon, a lecture, a meeting with the councils. No one saw the anguish of heart behind the marblelike features. In the study, door shut, the man wrestled with his sorrow. In the streets and in the pulpit he masked his grief and went on as before.

Viret, who had been completely overcome with the death of his own first wife three years before, wrote Calvin, "Wonderfully and incredibly have I been . . . informed . . . how you, with a heart so broken . . . , have attended to all your duties even better than hitherto. . . . Go on then as you have begun . . . and I pray God most earnestly . . . that you may receive daily greater comfort, and be strengthened more and more."

Life in the house on Canon Street moved along in its daily routine. Brother Antoine and his family were usually there. So was Idelette's daughter Judith until she married. Calvin had a hunchbacked servant,

Pierre, to take care of his needs. But how different the house was without the peace and serenity of Idelette. Even from her bed she had spread that peacefulness about her.

"My wife, a woman of rare qualities, died a year and a half ago," Calvin was to write in 1550, "and I have now willingly chosen to lead a solitary life."

29

"You yourself know, or at least ought to know, what I am; that, at all events, I am one to whom the law of my heavenly Master is so dear, that the cause of no man on earth will induce me to flinch from maintaining it with a pure conscience."

The man who spoke these forceful words meant every one of them. He had been asked to return to Geneva. He now was working to make Geneva a city in which the law of his heavenly Master was supreme. This meant a battle, in fact, a whole string of battles. The fourteen stormy years from 1541 to 1555 were filled with these battles. Calvin fought them also with his pen when he wrote against heresy and persecution outside of Geneva.

The man who fought these battles was already famous in his own time. He was so forceful and brilliant that people either followed his leadership eagerly or hated him bitterly. In Calvin's home town of Noyon, the canons of the cathedral staged a public procession celebrating his death when they heard a false rumor of it in 1551. Later the Calvin house on the corn-market square was burned down in anger. Somehow, miraculously, it had escaped a fire which destroyed most of the center of Noyon in 1552. In the French town of Lyons Calvin was reported dead "ten times over," so eager were his foes to have him out of the way. The Church of Rome considered him its chief enemy.

A keen, determined fighter—was this all there was to John Calvin? Many knew better. They knew he was a friend to thousands for Christ's sake. They saw how he chose to live humbly, almost in poverty. They knew that in the thick of trouble he could still delight in the beauty of God's world. Calvin could laugh and play games. And though his days were crowded with the troubles of Geneva, he kept his eyes on the whole world. He reached out to influence that world for his Master. Far from delighting in battles, he worked all his life to bring peace and unity among the new Protestant churches. To see John Calvin honestly, one must see him this way before watching him fight his battles to make the Church of Jesus Christ pure and true to the Word.

John Calvin was a friend, an honest, generous, wholehearted friend. All his life he had close personal friends. Besides, he was a friend to many brothers in Christ, some of whom never met the man who sent them letters of comfort and inspiration.

Farel and Viret—these were Calvin's closest friends in the last twenty-eight years of his life. Farel, the older man, the thundering, impetuous, fearless dynamo. Viret, the steady, kindly, learned brother, two years younger than Calvin. "I do not think that there has ever been, in ordinary life, a circle of friends so sincerely bound to each other as we have been in our ministry." So Calvin wrote in his dedication of the commentary on Titus.

Calvin dedicated this commentary to "two eminent servants of Christ, William Farel and Peter Viret, dearly beloved brethren and colleagues in the work of our Lord." He had chosen to dedicate the book on Titus to them because, as Titus was given "the task of putting the finishing hand to that building which Paul had begun in Crete," so in the church of Geneva "I occupy nearly the same position with regard to you." What Farel and Viret had begun in Geneva "at great risk . . . so well and so successfully," Calvin was now working to complete. Speaking of the fast friendship between them, Calvin continues, "I have been a fellow pastor here with both of you; and so far was there from being any appearance of envy, that you and I seemed to be one." Calvin wrote the dedication eight months after the death of Idelette, when friends meant more to him than ever.

The three friends did not always agree. Viret, the kindly one, was not often involved in arguments, but Farel and Calvin minced no words with each other. Yet, beneath the bluntness of their language lay the firm foundation of their friendship and their common bond as ministers of Christ.

Calvin was also quick to help his friends, no matter how busy he was. When he heard that Farel needed a new housekeeper, he found him one—a woman "pious, upright, careful, and advanced in years." Apparently Calvin thought it necessary that the woman be "advanced in years" if she was to keep house for an old bachelor. The most serious disagreement Calvin ever had with his friend came in 1558 over the marriage of Farel to a young girl, the daughter of another of Farel's housekeepers.

When Viret's first wife died in 1546 and "the whole world" appeared to him "nothing but a burden," Calvin urged his friend to come to Geneva for rest and recovery. "Make haste . . . and gather heart again with us," he wrote Viret. "People from your quarter say you are half dead." Another time the rumor came that Viret was dying from poisoning. At Calvin's command, Textor, the doctor, was ready to rush to Lausanne "on fleet horses." But the good news came that the rumor was untrue.

And then there was the matter of finding a second wife for Viret. Interestingly, Viret began to work on this only three months after the death of his first wife. Calvin helpfully wrote a friend in another city, "You know that our brother Viret is about to marry. I am in as great anxiety about it as he is. We have plenty of wives here . . . but yet there has not appeared a single one with whom I should feel at all satisfied. . . . If you have noticed anyone in your quarter who appears . . . likely to suit him, . . . please let me know."

Viret found his own second wife, Calvin pronounced the wedding benediction, and in the years that followed he often sent his greetings to the "three little daughters" born in the Viret home.

Farel and Viret were Calvin's close friends during his later years as a pastor. But his childhood companions and the acquaintances of student days in Paris and Orléans—these were still his friends, too. Many of them came to Geneva or wrote letters to Calvin.

One of the de Hangest boys, with whom Calvin had grown up in Noyon, wrote that he wanted above all things to come to Geneva to live.

François Daniel, the close friend of law school days in Orléans, the man who had never broken with the Church of Rome despite his Protestant leanings and despite Calvin's urging—this man was writing Calvin in 1559, twenty-eight years after studying law with him. Daniel's son had come to Geneva. Calvin helped him there and wrote the boy's father, his classmate, "For the love I bear to you, . . . I am wholly at your service." Along with the letter went some gold pieces for François Daniel's daughters, "as a kind of New Year's gift," because of Calvin's gratitude for what François had done for him many years earlier.

Another friend of student days came to live next door to Calvin on Canon Street. He was Michel Cop, brother of the Nicolas who was rector at the University of Paris when he and Calvin were forced to flee from that city. Michel Cop became a forceful, outspoken pastor in Geneva.

And the family of Guillaume Budé, the greatest new thinker of France, came to Geneva, too. The man himself had died in 1540, but Madame Budé with her daughter and three sons came to live in Calvin's city. John, one of the sons, became a close friend of Calvin, and was an important member of the Geneva councils.

A month after the death of Idelette, "eight French gentlemen" arrived in Geneva and asked permission to stay. One of them was handsome Theodore Beza, who as a twelve-year-old boy had lived in the house

160

of Wolmar, the Greek professor, in the French city of Bourges. Calvin had met the boy there.

Theodore Beza had been reared by two rich unmarried uncles. He had become a fine scholar. He had also lived wildly. Like Calvin, Beza was educated in law but at the same time held some church benefices which one of his uncles got for him.

After a critical illness, Beza became serious, turned toward the Protestant faith, and decided to go to Geneva. The boy of Wolmar's house was becoming a man ready for use in Christ's church. The academy of Lausanne called Beza to be professor of Greek, and he accepted this position. Before Beza left for Lausanne, he married a French girl in the church of Saint Pierre with Pastor John Calvin officiating. In the early years of his renewed friendship with Calvin, Beza wrote another pastor, "I have received the friendship of Calvin, Viret. . . . When I think that these are my friends, so far from feeling any inconvenience from exile, I may adopt the saying of Themistocles, 'I had been lost had I not become an exile.'"

The exile Beza came back to Geneva in 1559. He returned as a pastor, as rector of the university Calvin founded, and as Calvin's right-hand man. It was Beza who wrote a life of Calvin, who collected his letters, and who was head of Geneva's church for forty years after Calvin died.

Calvin's friends included Christian leaders with whom he did not always agree in doctrine. There was Bucer of Strasbourg, who was forced into exile and became professor at England's Cambridge University. Bucer was disheartened and lonely in England. Its chillier climate often made him ill. "Would that I were able in some measure to lighten the sufferings of your heart, and those cares with which I see you are tortured," Calvin wrote the friend who had been his Strasbourg father. Bucer was, on many points, a Lutheran. He had been one of Luther's companions at the famous Diet of Worms.

Heinrich Bullinger, the talented successor to Zwingli at Zurich, was a friend of Calvin. In many letters they talked of the church of Christ, of its doctrines and its problems. They spoke firmly and strongly to each other when they did not agree. But the bond of friendship between them was strong.

And the mild Melanchthon, who in his older years brooded sadly over the trouble and fighting among the Lutherans—he was also Calvin's friend. Sometimes Calvin scolded him severely for his unwillingness to take a firm stand among the Lutherans. Calvin begged Melanchthon to declare himself in favor of the Reformed view of the Lord's Supper. Melanchthon always retreated from doing this. He might have brought the Lutheran and the Reformed churches closer together. But he refused. And with all this at stake, Calvin still spoke yearningly of him.

In April of 1560, when Melanchthon was sixty-three years and sixty-three days old, he died in Wittenberg and was buried next to Luther in the floor of the Castle Church. To the end he had kept his mouth sealed. Calvin, writing amidst the continuing argument between the Lutheran and the Reformed churches, cried out, "O Philip Melanchthon, I appeal to thee as my witness! Thou now livest with Christ in the presence of God, and waitest for us to share with thee that blessed rest. Wearied with labor, oppressed with many cares, a hundred times didst thou express thy wish to live and die with me. I too a thousand times wished that we could live together. Assuredly thou wouldst then have been stronger to begin the fight. . . ." Much as Calvin longed for unity among the Protestant churches, he also loved the man whose silence had made that unity less possible.

Not all of Calvin's friends were great people. Wherever he went, to Ferrara, to Strasbourg, to other Swiss towns, he made friends. Where he did not go himself, he sent his messages by letter. No one knows how many friends in Christ received a message from their friend in Geneva. Over and over the pastor of Geneva stood beside the persecuted common folk of France in the words of his letters, which were delivered to them in prison. Many a Christian went to the stake strengthened by the words of a man he had never seen, a man who had never seen him, either.

The refugees who flooded Geneva at the rate of a thousand each year found that Calvin was their best friend. He found homes for them. He persuaded the councils to set up a cloth-manufacturing business to give the refugees work. He established church services in different languages for different refugee groups—English, Italian, Spanish, and Flemish. He was never too busy or too sick to find someone a house, a wife, a servant, a job.

Such a friend was the man on Canon Street in Geneva—a famous warrior for Christ, but just as much, a faithful friend for Christ's sake.

30

"Neither the table at which we eat, nor the bed on which we sleep, is our own. . . . Where, then, do these rumors come from? My acquaintances well know . . . that I do not possess a foot of land. . . . I never had money sufficient to purchase an acre." Yet an enemy had spread the rumor that Calvin had paid thousands of dollars for an estate.

Even the pope in Rome knew that Calvin was poor and that he wanted to be poor. Pius IV, who followed Paul III, said when Calvin died, "The strength of that heretic came from the fact that money was nothing to him." In the Church of Rome such an attitude was unheard of.

One day—so goes the story—Cardinal Sadolet passed incognito through Geneva. He was the cardinal who had tried to coax Geneva back to Rome while Calvin had been exiled from the city. Sadolet wanted to have a look at the famous Protestant who had written the eloquent reply for Geneva. He stood amazed in front of the simple house on Canon Street. Did the famous Calvin live in this little place? He knocked. Calvin himself, in a plain black robe, answered the door. Sadolet was dumbfounded. Where were the servants who should have been scurrying about to do their master's bidding? Even the bishops of Rome lived in mansions surrounded by wealth and servants. Archbishops and cardinals lived in palaces, like kings. And here was the most famous man in the whole Protestant church, in a little dark house, answering his own door.

"I am truly rich," said Calvin, "because I am abundantly satisfied with my slender means." The "slender means" did not always cover the cost of entertaining guests and paying for medicines and helping needy people at the door. Yet Calvin would not accept the councils' help without repaying them. In 1546, the council minutes record a sickness of Calvin, "who hath no resources." The councils sent him ten crowns. "On his recovery," further say the minutes, "he returns the money to the councils, who cause it to be expended in the purchase of a tun of wine for him, thus leaving him no alternative but to accept it." Still Calvin had the last word. He laid out ten crowns from his salary "for the relief of the poorest ministers." Yet this same year he was in debt for the illness of his second child, the little daughter who died. The next year the Little Council adopted a motion, "Resolved to present to Calvin all the furniture belonging to the city that is in his house." Calvin was now eating from his own table and sleeping on his own bed!

One year, to meet mounting expenses of his sickness, Calvin asked to borrow twenty-five dollars. When he was ready to repay the councils, they refused to accept the money. So he told them "that he would never again enter the pulpit" if they would not allow him to repay their help, and he rejected part of the salary due him. Another time, when the ministers requested Calvin to ask the councils for a raise in their salaries, he proposed that the councils lower his salary and share that money evenly with the other pastors.

Enemies, searching for something to criticize, made up false evidence to prove that Calvin was rich. In his preface to the commentary on Psalms, Calvin answered them. "If there are any whom, in my lifetime, I cannot persuade that I am neither rich nor moneyed, my death will show it at last." It did. Everything Calvin owned did not amount to more than about two hundred twenty-five dollars. Had he lived longer, he would have been still poorer, since he had refused to accept his last quarter's salary. I have not earned it, he said, so why should I receive it?

"Satisfied with my humble condition, I have ever delighted in a life of poverty." In this, too, John Calvin followed the example of his Master. Yet Calvin could be delighted with riches of the kind that money cannot buy. He delighted in the beauty God had put into His world. "The little singing birds are singing of God; the beasts cry unto Him; the elements are in awe of Him; the mountains echo His name; the waves and fountains cast their glances at Him; grass and flowers laugh out to Him." These are the riches of which Calvin speaks in the preface written for Olivétan's New Testament in 1535.

Calvin had a sense of humor. He made good puns. He could laugh with his friends. And sometimes, before his illnesses stopped him, he took time for recreation. He walked in his garden overlooking the lake. He rode horseback through the countryside with his fellow ministers. Or he went to his brother Antoine's country house.

Occasionally he found time for games. He played

quoits, a game like horseshoes or ringtoss, played with flat iron discs. He liked to challenge others to a key-throwing game: the player sliding a key ring nearest to the opposite side of the table was the winner. Sometimes Calvin played bowls, an indoor game like tenpins. Calvin was playing bowls one Sunday afternoon when a visitor came to call on him.

But usually Calvin found no time for recreation. Like a captain on a ship in rough seas, he was too busy sailing the ship safely toward port.

That ship was the whole Protestant church, not just the church of Geneva. Geneva had problems enough to overload a pastor, but Calvin kept watch over the rest of the world, too. Governments and battles and treaties and political intrigues—he knew the details of them all. They were important to him not in themselves, but because they affected the whole church of Christ, which was always Calvin's chief concern.

To build up the church, Calvin wrote letters to kings and princes. To rulers who showed sympathy for the Reformation faith, he dedicated commentaries—Hebrews to the king of Poland, Acts to the kings of Denmark and Sweden, four epistles to a German duke. He wrote a catechism for the Protestants in Austria. He sent a long list of reforms to Emperor Charles, who was holding another imperial diet at Spires.

Calvin was especially active in writing to England during the seven-year reign of the boy king, Edward VI, who died when he was sixteen. The duke of Somerset, uncle of the young king, was the lord protector who ruled with several other regents. Thomas Cranmer,

167

archbishop of Canterbury, was another of the regents. He had helped Henry VIII change the religion of England—all because of a divorce which the pope would not grant to Henry. Now Cranmer was busy championing the Reformation and changing the Church of England.

Calvin was thrilled to see another great country coming into the Protestant group. With his pen he did what he could to strengthen the Church of England. In 1548 he dedicated his commentary on First Timothy to the duke of Somerset. With it he sent a long letter suggesting reforms for the English church. May the Lord make you "a repairer of His temple," wrote Calvin, "so that the times of the king, your nephew, may be compared to those of Josiah," the boy king of the Old Testament. The duke was grateful for Calvin's writings. The duchess sent Calvin a ring.

Two and a half years later Calvin sent a minister as special messenger to the fourteen-year-old king. The pastor brought copies of Calvin's two latest commentaries, those on Isaiah and on the epistles of James, Peter, John, and Jude. They were dedicated to "His Serene Highness, Edward VI, King of England, a Truly Christian Prince."

A year before Edward VI died, Calvin sent him another gift of writing. This was a little book, *Four Sermons of Master John Calvin.* In the letter that went with the book, Calvin speaks eloquently. "It is indeed a great thing to be a king," he says, "and . . . over such a country; but I have no doubt that you reckon it beyond comparison better to be a Christian. It is therefore an invaluable privilege that God has granted you, Sire, to be a Christian king."

To the kings of France Calvin could not speak that way. Under Francis I and his son Henry II, persecutions continued. In the forty-four years that these two kings ruled, fifty thousand Protestants were killed. Thousands more went into exile. At Meaux, where the beginnings of a French reformation had been strong thirty years earlier, fourteen men were hanged on a circle of gallows in the market square and burned to death. A Paris professor was left six weeks in a narrow pit in which he could neither stand nor lie, and then he was burned. The hardworking, devout Waldensian people, who lived in the mountain valleys of southeast France, were horribly massacred. A cardinal had told the king lies about them. In 1545 three thousand of them—men, women, and children—were killed. Forty women fled into a barn. Soldiers set fire to the straw-filled barn and as the women rushed out, they were speared by the pikes, the bayonetlike weapons of the soldiers. Waldensian villages and peaceful farms were destroyed. Some of the people wandered, starving, in the forests. Others escaped to Switzerland to tell the terrible news.

These persecutions stirred Calvin deeply. He wrote many letters to influential people. He made two trips to the other Swiss churches, gathering money for the refugees, persuading the churches and cantons to write strong protests to the king of France. The French king replied curtly that the cantons of Switzerland would kindly mind their own business and he would mind his.

In the midst of French persecutions and German church quarrels, Calvin was at work to bring some unity among the churches, at least among the Swiss followers of Zwingli and himself. He had hoped to reach agreement with the Lutherans. But this had become less and less possible with Luther's unpredictable temper, Melanchthon's unwillingness to take a firm stand, and the rise of radical leaders in the troubled Lutheran states after the death of Luther. Calvin now worked hopefully with the leaders of the Zwinglians.

The stumbling block to agreement was the interpretation of the Lord's Supper. In 1548 Calvin wrote Bullinger, the leader of the Zwinglians. I may hold that Christ is present in the Lord's Supper in a fuller way than you hold Him to be, wrote Calvin, but "we will not, on that account, cease to hold the same Christ, and to be one in Him." Then he sent twenty-four articles on the subject of the Lord's Supper, to be used as a basis for discussion.

Six weeks after the death of Idelette it was a comfort for Calvin to go with Farel to Zurich to talk with Bullinger and the others. Unity seemed near. Calvin had received a letter from Bullinger and had replied, "I have scarcely ever received anything more pleasant from you. . . . I am very glad that hardly anything . . . hinders us from agreement now even in words. . . . It shall never be owing to me that we do not unite in a solid peace, as we all unanimously profess the same Christ."

The evidence of this unity was the Zurich *Consensus* of 1549, written largely, if not entirely, by Calvin. In the two years following, the Swiss churches put their signatures to the *Consensus*. At least in his adopted country, Calvin could give thanks for some unity among the churches. Two years after Calvin's death, in the famous *Helvetic Confession of 1566*, the union of the Swiss churches was completed, as the pastor of Geneva always had hoped that it would be.

In England, Archbishop Cranmer had hopes of church union, too. Many of the English leaders during the reign of Edward VI were sympathetic to Calvin's teachings. Bucer was also in England and had much influence until his death. Cranmer wanted to hold a synod to discuss differences in doctrine among Protestants. He wrote to Calvin, to Bullinger of the Zwinglians, to Melanchthon of the Lutherans. "I pray you to deliberate among yourselves as to the means by which this synod can be assembled with the greatest convenience," he wrote. At that time the Church of Rome was holding its Council of Trent. "Shall we neglect to call together a godly synod . . . for restoring and propagating the truth?" asked Cranmer in 1552.

The next year England's boy king died. The synod was never held. Cranmer himself died at the stake during the reign of Bloody Mary. But Calvin, to whom the unity of Protestant churches was always dear, had replied to the archbishop's proposal for a synod. "So much does this concern me," Calvin had said, "that, could I be of any service, I would not grudge to cross even ten seas, if need were, on account of it. . . . Would that I were as able as I am willing."

Calvin, the faithful friend and comforter, the humble man to whom money was nothing, the far-seeing pastor who watched over Christ's churches everywhere and worked for unity among them—this man was also an unflinching warrior in establishing the kingdom of his Master and in making his Master's church pure and holy. He was no born fighter, as were Luther and Farel. He hated every minute of battle. But when the work of the Lord demanded fighting, Calvin was ready.

31

One enemy after another appeared in Geneva to do battle with Calvin.

First, and unexpectedly, came the twenty-six-year-old scholar whom Calvin himself had appointed rector of the high school.

This Sebastian Castellio was making a translation of the New Testament. He wanted it to be a popular, down-to-earth translation. He asked Calvin to recommend it for publication. To Calvin the translation seemed crude and at some points inaccurate. But he did not have time in his busy schedule to argue for hours with Castellio over each unacceptable phrase. Castellio was peeved that Calvin would not recommend the translation wholeheartedly.

Some things about Castellio's doctrines and beliefs Calvin could not recommend, either. The young rector claimed that the Song of Solomon was not an inspired book of the Bible. It is only a very human description of one of Solomon's love affairs, said Castellio. He did not agree with the words "descended into hell" in the Apostles' Creed. Neither did he accept the doctrine of election—that God, before the world began, has chosen those who will be saved.

All of this had been tolerated until Castellio applied to become one of Geneva's pastors. His rector's salary was too low, he said. The Little Council approved the application, but final power to recommend pastors belonged to the church consistory. Under Calvin's leadership, the consistory refused Castellio's application because he held objectionable views and doctrines. Instead, the consistory offered to ask the councils to raise the rector's salary.

Angry at being refused entrance into the ministry, Castellio resigned his rectorship. Calvin offered to help Castellio by sending letters of recommendation to Viret in Lausanne. "I am truly sorry on his own account," wrote Calvin. "Help him to the utmost of your power."

But Castellio found no teaching position in Lausanne and returned to Geneva. One afternoon in 1544 he appeared in the weekly meeting of ministers and laymen. Sixty of them were listening to Calvin explain Paul's words, "But in all things approving ourselves as the ministers of God. . . ."

Up popped Castellio and interrupted. You ministers of Geneva are not like Paul, he said sarcastically. You obey your own whims, you get angry quickly, you waste your time sporting and drinking, your lives are wild and loose. You could not be more unlike Paul, he scoffed. Calvin made no reply. Controlling himself, he closed the Bible and left the room.

The Little Council took up the matter of Castellio's public insult to the ministers of Geneva. They ordered Castellio to leave the city. He left with letters of recommendation from Calvin and the ministers, who were glad to recommend Castellio as a scholar even though they could not approve his admission to the ministry. But Castellio carried with him a bitter hatred of Calvin—a hatred expressed once more when he published a book denouncing the burning of Servetus some years later.

The next enemy to challenge Calvin was Pierre Ameaux, whose wife was one of Geneva's notorious Libertines. She took so much liberty, in fact, that she lived in free love with a variety of men. It seems that Calvin advised the couple to separate, but the Little Council was slow to sanction Pierre's formal divorce from his unfaithful wife. At last the divorce took place, and the woman sat six months in prison. But Pierre Ameaux was disgusted with the delay of a year and a half. And he had another reason for fretting. His business was the manufacture of playing cards, and since the return of Calvin—with laws being enforced—there was a decided slump in the sale of his cards.

One night Ameaux invited four friends to dinner. Warmed by his wine, he became eloquent against the French preacher of Canon Street. He complained loud and long while his four friends nodded in agreement. Two-faced friends that they were, they promptly reported the whole oration to the councils, of which Ameaux was a member. Ameaux was arrested and put in prison to await sentence. Calvin asked that the sentence be lenient. But let it be public, he requested, so that the people may be warned. Instead the Little Council decided to have Ameaux apologize to them at a closed meeting.

This action irritated Calvin. The whole city knew about the Ameaux incident. Other offenses were often punished by public humiliation in the streets. And now this man got off with an apology behind closed doors. Backed by the other ministers, Calvin demanded a public punishment for a man who was known to have defied the doctrines of the church and to have slandered one of its ministers.

Enemies of Calvin saw their chance to stir up trouble. Soon the mutterings and threats grew louder. Citizens oiled their muskets. The disorder was worst across the river in the Saint Gervais district where Ameaux lived. To quiet the people, the Little Council marched in procession over the bridge and stood at attention while a gallows was set up in Saint Gervais Square.

Soon the Little Council passed its reconsidered verdict. Pierre Ameaux, having spoken against God, the councils, and Master Calvin, was to walk through the city, "your head bare and a lighted torch of wax in your hands," was to kneel "in front of the town hall, in front of us seated in tribunal, saying and confessing in a loud and clear voice that against God, truth, and right, you declared that Master John Calvin had proclaimed false doctrine. Then you will be led through the . . . city . . . to the three principal public squares . . . and in each of these three places you will make a similar confession on your knees, the torch in your hand, to serve as an example to others."

It was April 5, 1546, when Pierre Ameaux did as he was ordered. The curious crowds gathered to watch—and to remember.

People soon realized that Calvin expected the councils to enforce the law on everyone. Perhaps it was a comfort to the poor to know that money, high society, and council membership did not give any man freedom to break the law. It was no comfort to those well-to-do citizens known as Libertines. They hated Calvin for the discipline he was trying to bring to their corrupt city. They hated him because he was a foreigner. The Libertines fought Calvin under cover and in the open. They fought him by siding with every new enemy who appeared to challenge him. Other enemies came and went, but it was fourteen years before the Libertines were defeated.

One Libertine family especially hated Calvin for what he was trying to do. This was the family Favré, a wealthy old family, fond of its pleasures. François, the father, convicted two or three times of adultery, had said he wished he were a syndic so that he could reopen the houses of ill fame in Geneva. Gaspard, one of the Favré sons, also had been in prison for immorality. When he was released, he spitefully gathered some of his rowdy friends and played a noisy game outside the church where Calvin was preaching. There was another son, John, who at his own wedding mockingly shook his head at the point where he should have answered, "I do."

But the Favré daughter, Francesca, was the worst of them all. What a woman she was! Her language was filthy, and she was defiant of all authority. Yet Francesca had married Ami Perrin, a councilman and captain general of the city militia.

In March of 1546, just before Ameaux made his public apology, Francesca and her husband Perrin danced at a wedding reception with a syndic named Corna and others. Years before Calvin had come to Geneva, the city had made laws against dancing. Now, with the urging of the church consistory, the laws were being enforced.

The syndic Corna apologized sincerely when he

was brought before the Little Council. But Francesca screamed and raged when she was brought in to answer for her dancing. "Pig, low-down liar, coarse swineherd" were some of the milder words she used against Calvin and the councilmen. The bailiffs had to drag Francesca out in the middle of her tantrum. Her husband, Ami Perrin, suddenly remembered he had to make a trip to Lyons, and so for the moment he dodged his punishment. Francesca was in jail a little while, but the matron let her out. How she hated Calvin! He had better watch out, she threatened, or he would "stir up a slumbering fire" and be kicked out of the city again.

Calvin tried several times to make peace with the Favré family, especially with Ami Perrin—who had been one of the messengers sent to Strasbourg to bring him back to Geneva. Perrin loved the loose and easy life. And yet, if his "monstrous fury" of a wife had not egged him on, he might have been persuaded. In a firm but pleading letter to Perrin, Calvin told him he was not bothered by Francesca's threats. "I did not come back to Geneva for leisure or gain," he wrote, "nor would it grieve me if I am forced to leave it. The . . . safety of church and state made me willing to return, . . . and I will lay aside that devoted attachment to this place only with my last breath." Urging Perrin to realize that the laws must be enforced fairly, Calvin pleaded, "May the Lord discover to you how greatly even the stripes of a sincere friend are to be preferred to the treacherous flattery of others."

But the anger of Ami Perrin and of his wife's family continued to burn. Two other men stepped forward to become Libertine leaders with Perrin.

177

One was Philibert Berthelier. His father had been a famous patriot who died fighting for Geneva's freedom. Philibert was no such great man. He was flashy and headstrong. The other man in the trio of Libertine leaders was handsome Pierre Vandel. Vandel loved to appear in public surrounded by valets and admirers, with his fingers full of gold rings and his chest covered with gold chains. He, too, had been in prison a few times for his wild behavior and insolent talk to the consistory.

These three—Perrin, Berthelier, Vandel—led the city's opposition to the order and purity Calvin was working to establish. They took every chance to oppose Calvin. In 1547 it was on the matter of slashed breeches. For the annual parade and target-shooting festival Ami Perrin wanted to have his militiamen decked out in short tight breeches, slashed on the side. He asked that the Council of Two Hundred decide about the breeches. Perrin expected to have more support from the Two Hundred than from the Little Council. Calvin spoke at the meeting. He was not arguing against the slashed breeches, he said, but was pointing out the direction in which such immodesty and luxury would lead. The Council of Two Hundred decided against the slashed breeches.

Ami Perrin, whom Calvin called "our comic Caesar," then "hastily set out on a journey . . . to avoid being present at the public parade" where his militiamen would not be marching in the new breeches.

Perrin had lost the battle of the slashed breeches. But he and his helpers were not yet through with Calvin.

32

The discontent smoldered along, waiting to burst again into flames.

The consistory did its work faithfully. Each of the twelve elders kept careful watch in his district. On Thursday mornings those accused by the consistory of breaking the city laws were brought before the Little Council to be sentenced. There was the man who stayed home and played cards during the Sunday sermon. And the fellows who laughed aloud in church and created a disturbance. And the citizen who heard a donkey bray and said sarcastically, "He chants a fine psalm." This last man was sent out of the city for three months. And then there was the never-ending array of drunkards, petty thieves, quarrelers and fighters, adulterers, and other offenders.

The city famous for wickedness and vice had a long way to go before it would appear to be a congregation of God's people. Often the councils acted indecisively. Always it was Calvin and his fellow ministers who urged, reproached, denounced, and pointed the way to a city and a church according to the Word.

For a while the taverns were closed. Instead, eating and drinking places called *abbayes* were set up. In the *abbayes* the French Bible was always on display.

No customer would be served food unless he first had prayed. The *abbayes* closed at nine in the evening.

But the reforming of Geneva was a long struggle.

In July of 1547 Francesca Perrin had another tussle with the consistory. Called before the ministers and elders to explain some misbehavior, she poured her choicest language upon the minister Abel Poupin. Then, to escape the sentence of the Little Council which was likely to follow, Francesca decided to leave town for a while. On her way to the city gate she spied the minister Poupin walking in the narrow street. Spurring her horse, she attempted to run him down. Failing this, she flung some coarse words over her shoulder and galloped off.

The next day an anonymous letter appeared mysteriously in the pulpit of Saint Pierre. It was written in a kind of dialect which few people of Geneva could speak or write. "Great Potbelly," it began, addressing the minister Poupin whose name meant "chubby." "You and your companions would do better to hold your tongues. . . . If you drive us too far, no one will protect you. . . . You will curse the hour you ever left your monkhood. . . . When one has endured too much, one takes revenge. . . . We will not have so many masters. Mark my words."

One of the few who could write and speak the Savoy dialect of the pulpit letter was Jacques Gruet, a former canon, who had been suspected of starting the poison plot against Viret and Farel before Calvin came to Geneva.

Gruet lived in a house by himself and was known for his immoral living. When the councils searched the house, they found some letters and writings in which Gruet scoffed at the church and state. It seemed he had written some things that smacked of treason. Under the common torture procedures of that day, Gruet "confessed" to writing the anonymous letter in the pulpit. Though not unanimously, the councils sentenced him "to have his head cut off above the shoulders, and his body fastened to the gallows and his head nailed above." According to the laws of his day, Jacques Gruet had received a just sentence. Three years after his execution, there was found in a crack in the wall of his house a twenty-four-page writing containing lewd talk against Christ, the virgin Mary, and the apostles. Christ was called, among other things, a crazy good-for-nothing, the virgin Mary was called a harlot, and the apostles were low-down rascals.

Actually, Calvin had little to do with the Gruet affair. But the people were stirred up by it. They associated it with Calvin's reforming of the city. More and more they were swayed by the Libertines.

One December day in 1547 the Council of Two Hundred was to meet. Calvin, on his way to speak to them, heard shouting and fighting going on in the courtyard of the town hall. He hurried toward it and found the councilmen waving their swords and scuffling wildly among themselves. The frail man in the black robe pushed into the middle of the fracas, shouting, "If you must shed blood, start with mine." Friends "dragged and seized me hither and thither, lest I should suffer injury." Amazed and a little ashamed, the angry councilmen went muttering into the council chamber. Here Calvin spoke to them long and earnestly.

But he was not deceived that his words had any great effect. It was "like telling a story to the deaf," he said. Dejected and disappointed, he wrote Viret, "Their wickedness has reached such a pitch, that I despair of holding this church any longer. Believe me, I am undone and broken, unless God stretch forth His hand to me." And to Farel, "May the Lord hear your incessant prayers on our behalf."

Perrin and his comrades rubbed their hands in satisfaction. It was spring 1549 and the elections had brought more Libertines into the councils. In the Council of Two Hundred they now matched the supporters of Calvin. Though they did not do quite that well in the Little Council, they had greater strength there, too. Perrin was elected a syndic, no less. He was flushed with victory.

The Libertines grew bolder. Calvin walked the streets, surrounded by insults. Even children taunted him by taking letters from his name and calling him Cain. People called their dogs, "Here, Calvin. Here, boy!" One day a rude group jostled him on the bridge that crossed the icy Rhone. It was all like the days of 1538 when he had been ordered to leave the city.

This was the spring when Idelette lay dying in the house on Canon Street, while the Libertine hatred against Calvin was reaching a new high.

Attacked on every side, left alone by the death of his wife—"Believe me, I am undone and broken, unless the Lord stretch forth His hand to me."

Two new enemies, both of them ex-monks, turned up to attack Calvin's theology. The Libertines welcomed their help. First, in 1551, came Jerome Bolsec, "who, having thrown off the monk's cowl, is become one of those strolling physicians." Bolsec also posed as an expert in theology. He criticized Calvin's theology to others, though he did not confront Calvin himself. One Friday the pastor of a nearby village preached. In the discussion period after the sermon, Bolsec stood up to denounce the doctrine of election. It is nonsense, he said. A detestable piece of folly. You make God a tyrant. Why, if God has decided everything from the beginning, He is responsible for sin itself. This Calvin, who teaches you these things, is an impostor. You are crazy to follow his leading.

Unnoticed, Calvin had arrived at the church in time for the discussion. He stood in the back of the room, listening to Bolsec's tirade. Then, to the surprise of the ex-monk who did not think him present, Calvin stepped forward to refute Bolsec, and defend the doctrine of election. With his usual memory, he quoted fully from the Bible and from church fathers like Augustine. In an argument from Scripture, could anyone stand before Calvin? The Little Council decided to order Bolsec out of the city.

In his old age and from his slight contact with Calvin, Bolsec turned out a book on the life of Geneva's reformer. Of all the books written by Calvin's enemies, this one was probably the most malicious—filled with lies, accusations, and imaginations.

Once again, in 1552, the Little Council met to hear debates on God's election. This time it was a native Genevan, a monk who had turned hermit for a while, who would lead the opposition. Zeraphin Trolliet had joined the Libertines, and was now ready to prove that Calvin in his *Institutes* made God the author of sin, and was therefore teaching false doctrine in the church of Geneva.

It was a long, drawn-out affair. Farel and Viret came to Geneva to stand with Calvin. The weary council clerk, quite unfamiliar with theology, wrote in his minutes, "Having heard . . . their replies, now often repeated. . . ." And the Little Council passed a verdict intended to keep everyone satisfied. It declared "the *Institutes* . . . to be well and holily done, and his [Calvin's] doctine to be God's doctrine." But it also declared Trolliet to be a good man and a good citizen. And so the thing was ended, but not settled.

Enemies in the streets and councils of Geneva. Trouble everywhere. The pastor of Canon Street fought them while his body called out for rest and peace. Sometimes his asthma gave way to attacks of pleurisy. He who had always to speak, in pulpit and lecture and council and at home, was forced to get his words out deliberately because breathing was not easy. Often Calvin could not sit or move comfortably because of severe hemorrhoids. Or the knifing pains of kidney and gallstones would torment him. If his hemorrhoids were bearable, he would take to his horse and gallop as fast as he could, hoping to jolt loose the stones for which his day knew no surgery. Headache—was he ever free from it? Sometimes he was blinded by the pain or kept awake all night. Many times Calvin ate only one meal a day. Cramps, indigestion, influenza were regular problems.

During these years of threats and insults and troubles, the sick man beset by enemies could not see the victory ahead. Slowly, slowly, the preaching and the catechism and the discipline were working their way into the hearts of many in Geneva. These people made no noise about it as the Libertines did in fighting Calvin. But they began to see that the way of Calvin, the way of the Word, with all the severity of its godly living as Calvin believed it—this was a better way than the loose bragging life of people like Perrin and his vixen wife Francesca.

Even in the councils where the Libertines had great strength, there was a slight majority who knew that Calvin had to stay in Geneva for Geneva's sake. These men might join in heckling the frail preacher and in refusing what he asked. They sometimes helped to throw obstacles in his way. They drove him to anger. But they knew they had to keep him. There was something about his utter honesty, his forceful character, his brilliant mind, and above all, his absolute dedication to his Master and his Master's Word. There was no one like him in Geneva—or anywhere else. No matter how much opposition the Libertines might stir up, the councils would never again ask John Calvin to leave their city.

And yet, with these glimmerings of victory, the greatest battle still lay ahead.

33

On a hill outside Geneva a man was burned at the stake.

Strangely, this was the second time the man was burned for heresy. Four months earlier he had been burned by the Church of Rome. But the followers of the pope had not been careful enough. The heretic had escaped from the prison where they held him.

And so, angry and frustrated, they had been able to burn only a straw-filled dummy—or was it a picture?—of their prisoner, along with five bales of his latest writing. It was left to the Protestant city of Geneva to burn the real man.

Michael Servetus, the man from Spain, the twice-burned heretic, had an early life quite like that of Calvin. He, too, was the son of a notary, the brother of a priest, a student of law, and a follower of the pope. Like Calvin, he began to study the Bible in its original languages while still a student of law. At the age of eighteen, Servetus came to the belief that cost him his life almost twenty-five years later.

God is not three persons, said Servetus. That makes Him a three-headed monster. "Not one word is found in the whole Bible about the Trinity or about its persons," insisted the Spaniard. Jesus is a man, and not the eternal Son of God. "The Holy Spirit is not a distinct being," but rather God's spirit sent into the world. At the age of twenty, Michael Servetus published his first book with these revolutionary ideas in it. From then on he was a marked man.

In Strasbourg, where the volume was printed in 1531, and in Basel, the town councils soon banned the book and forbade its sale. The Protestant leaders of these cities considered it blasphemy and error. Luther, Melanchthon, Bucer, Bullinger, and Zwingli spoke against it.

Servetus knew what the Church of Rome would say about his first book. When the news of it got over the mountains to Spain, the Supreme Council of the Spanish Inquisition ordered the author brought back to his native land, no matter what means had to be used. Promise him favors, lie to him, order him—do anything to bring Servetus back where we can get our hands on him, said the Supreme Council. It even sent his own brother, the priest, to persuade him to return.

What could Servetus do? The Protestants rejected him and banned his book. The Church of Rome would escort him straight to the stake. Servetus toyed with the idea of going to the newly discovered Americas. Then he found an easier solution. He changed his name to Michel de Villeneuve, after the town of his birth, and went undiscovered for twenty years.

Servetus was twenty-two years old when he turned up in Paris and made an appointment with John Calvin, then recently converted. For some reason, Servetus never came to the place agreed upon, though Calvin waited for him there, at the risk of his life.

In the next few years, the restless, brilliant Servetus did many things. He edited a world geography book for a publisher in Lyons. He studied medicine in Paris and is probably the first man to discover how blood circulates in the lungs. He lectured on geography and astrology. He reported an eclipse of Mars by the moon. He even ventured to predict from the stars what was going to happen to men and nations. For this and for speaking insolently to a professor, Servetus was brought to trial before the French parliament. He defended himself so successfully that he got off with only a stern reprimand, and with having his current writing on astrology banned. No one suspected who he really was.

Then for twelve peaceful years Servetus lived in the French town of Vienne, near Lyons. He edited books and practiced medicine. He was a model follower of Rome and a great friend of the arch-bishop, who never dreamed that Servetus thought the pope to be the "vilest of all beasts, most brazen of harlots." While Servetus continued this two-faced existence, he was busy with another book. John Calvin had called his masterpiece the *Institutes.* Servetus called his the *Restitutes,* as if he were now restoring the truth of the Christian religion to its purest form.

In 1546 and 1547, when he was thirty-five years old, Servetus corresponded with Calvin. Calvin answered courteously and sent Servetus a copy of his *Institutes.* The copy came back to him scribbled over with insulting comments. Servetus sent more long letters, thirty in all, in which he spoke condescendingly and sharply to Calvin. He also sent him a manuscript of his forthcoming *Restitutes.* But Calvin felt it was a waste of precious time to go on arguing with Servetus. He wrote him no more. In a letter to Farel he said, "Servetus has just sent me, together with his letter, a long volume of his ravings. If I consent he will come here, but I will not give my word, for should he come, if my authority is of any avail, I will not suffer him to get out alive." Yet Calvin, knowing who Servetus really was, made no attempt to reveal him to the Roman Catholic authorities in Vienne.

Six years later the *Restitutes* was printed secretly outside the city of Vienne. The two printers, brothers-in-law, were both men who had lived in Geneva. One was a former Libertine. The other was friendly to Calvin's ideas. The friendly one apparently did not realize what his Libertine brother-in-law had agreed to print. In place of his name, Servetus used only the initials M.S.V. (Michael Servetus Villeneuve) on the title page. But he had included in the back of the book the thirty letters he had written to Calvin.

At the same time, in the nearby city of Lyons, five Protestant ministers were lying in prison. They had just finished their study in Switzerland and were returning as missionaries to their native France. Three hours over the border they were discovered, seized, and imprisoned. The whole Protestant world was excited about their fate. Protest letters and messengers came in a stream from Swiss cities and churches. Calvin wrote, too. He also sent beautiful letters of comfort and encouragement to the five young preachers who were kept a year in prison before they were chained together and burned at the stake in May of 1553.

While the five young preachers waited in jail, and just after the publishing of Servetus' book, a Protestant of Geneva wrote to his Roman Catholic cousin who lived in Lyons. There was sharp feeling between them, especially with the five ministers in jail. The Catholic cousin of Lyons had often chided his Protestant cousin about the lack of church order and discipline in Geneva. Now the Protestant cousin had something very special to say in reply.

My dear cousin, wrote the Protestant of Geneva. Do not complain about our lack of church discipline in Geneva. Right in your own neighborhood there lives a heretic who blasphemes the Trinity and has just written a book full of heresy. Yet this man lives in honor among you, under the nose of the cardinal and the archbishop, while your prisons are full of innocent people. The heretic of whom I speak is Servetus, the Spaniard, known in Vienne as Michel de Villeneuve. He practices medicine there. Just to prove what I say, I am sending you the first four pages of his new book.

The Catholic cousin of Lyons went straight to the church authorities with the news. They called in Servetus, who swore up and down that he was only Michel de Villeneuve, a most faithful follower of Rome. The authorities needed more proof. They asked the Catholic cousin to write to Geneva to get it.

The Protestant cousin in Geneva replied to the request. "I did not suppose that the matter would go so far," he said honestly. "But since you have disclosed what I meant for you alone, God grant that this may . . . serve to purge Christianity of such filth, such deadly pestilence." Then he explained that to get further proof he had gone to Calvin, his good friend, who had some handwritten letters from Servetus. "But I can tell you I had no little trouble to get from Calvin what I am sending," he wrote, enclosing a few of the letters, the same letters that were printed in the back of the new book. The Protestant cousin had argued a long time with Calvin, pleading and explaining how embarrassed he would be if Calvin did not help him. "In the end he [Calvin] gave me what you see."

Did Calvin know that these original letters of Servetus would be turned over to the authorities and used against Servetus? Calvin himself later denied that he was active in turning over Servetus to the Church of Rome, and we have no reason to doubt his word. No matter how the letters were intended to be used, they became the clinching evidence against Servetus. In vain Servetus cried and cringed and lied to clear himself. The evidence was there. He was put into prison to await his sentence. It was early April 1553.

The prison had a garden on a terrace, high up from the street. The garden was always locked, but distinguished prisoners were allowed in it, because the prison had no decent bathroom facilities. The third morning that Servetus was in prison he got up at four o'clock, dressed, and then put on his velvet nightcap and fur bathrobe over his clothes. He asked the jailer for the key to the garden. Unsuspecting, the jailer gave it and went off to tend his vines. Servetus shed his bathrobe and nightcap under a tree, jumped from the garden onto a roof next to it, and from there dropped down into a courtyard. In the early dawn only a peasant woman saw him as he hurried through the streets and out of the city gate.

There was a frantic search for the missing prisoner. Then the city court of Vienne passed sentence and ordered it carried out in effigy. This was the first burning of Servetus, done in great solemnity, with a straw-filled dummy for a victim.

Four months later the real man arrived in Geneva. He found lodging at the Inn of the Golden Rose and asked his landlord to arrange a boat to take him across the lake toward Zurich.

It was Sunday. Everyone was expected in church. Servetus went, too. Someone recognized him there and told Calvin, who immediately asked the councils to arrest the visitor. The secretary of Calvin went to prison along with Servetus, because of the rule that an accuser had to stay in prison, too, until the charges he made were proved. The secretary offered to go in Calvin's place so that Calvin would not be detained in his daily work.

"On August the 13th [1553] . . . Michael Servetus was recognized by certain brothers, and it seemed good to make him a prisoner that he might no longer infect the world with his heresies and blasphemies, seeing that he was known to be incorrigible and hopeless." So read the minutes of the Geneva church consistory.

What possessed Servetus to come to Geneva?

He was on his way to Naples, Italy, to practice medicine—so he said at his trial. The road from Vienne to Naples certainly did not lie north through Geneva and Zurich. Why then did he come to Geneva, when he had so narrowly escaped the fire of the Church of Rome? Did Servetus hear from the Libertine who printed his *Restitutes* that Calvin was having trouble in Geneva? Did he know that Calvin's enemies hoped to overthrow him and his work? Yes, probably he had heard these things. Did he then count on these enemies to support him? Did he hope to spread his own doctrine in Geneva? Or was he just passing through, out of curiosity? No one knows.

Calvin drew up a document of thirty-nine accusations against Servetus. Then the trial began. It continued, off and on, for two and a half months. Some of it was in Latin writing between Calvin and Servetus. Some of it was in face-to-face argument.

The Libertines were delighted to side with this new enemy of Calvin. Ami Perrin sat in the chairman's seat of the Little Council. Berthelier, another Libertine leader, was an official in the proceedings. Servetus himself, far from crying and cringing as he had done before the court in Vienne, was cocky and disdainful of Calvin. He seemed very sure of himself. He hurled names and mockery at Calvin as if Calvin were the man accused. "Criminal, killer, wretch, liar, ridiculous dwarf, . . . do you believe yourself able to deafen the ears of the judges with your dog's barking?" Such was his language.

Calvin continued to advance proof for his thirty-nine accusations. The two men argued vehemently, on paper and in person. Though Servetus was more insulting and disdainful, Calvin, too, spoke in anger. His words cut like knives. He often spoke harshly. Calvin was filled with a mighty wrath against this man who brazenly denied that Christ was eternally God. This was the man who also arrogantly asserted that people are born innocent, that babies ought not to be baptized, and that men, not God, decide their own salvation. Could such a blaspheming heretic go unpunished, while thousands of faithful Protestants were being burned everywhere?

Servetus must be punished. The laws of the age said so. They were printed, black on white, in the *Codex of Justinian,* the standard civil lawbook still followed in the Holy Roman Empire. For the crime of denying the Trinity, said the *Codex,* the penalty is death.

34

But the power to sentence Servetus did not lie in the hands of Calvin.

It was completely in the hands of the Little Council of Geneva. And never had Calvin had as little influence over that council as he did in the months when Servetus was in prison.

These were the months of the death struggle with the Libertines over the question of excommunication. Berthelier, the Libertine leader, had been told by the consistory that he could not come to the Lord's Supper. In a drunken brawl he and some companions had chased one of the preachers to his doorstep. Now the Little Council boldly took to itself the power of the church and restored the right to communion to Berthelier. The Libertines were flushed with power. They were ready to challenge Calvin on this all-important matter which lay at the heart of his church government.

Calvin protested strongly. The Little Council, with Ami Perrin as chairman, overruled his protest. On the day before the September Lord's Supper, Calvin faced the twenty-five men in the council chamber. Trembling with emotion, he told them, "I swear rather to die than to have the Lord's Supper defiled. . . . I would rather be dead a hundred times than to commit such terrible mockery against Christ."

The next morning Calvin stood in the pulpit of Saint Pierre, unaware that after he had left the council chamber, a majority of the members had decided that Berthelier must not appear in church the next day.

This was one of the most dramatic moments in Calvin's life. "I asked that God would give me firmness and my prayer was answered," he told the hushed congregation before the Lord's Supper. "Therefore know that whatever may occur, I shall act according to the clearly revealed command of my

Master. Should there be anyone during the Lord's Supper which we are about to celebrate approaching the table of the Lord who has been denied this privilege by the elders, I shall take the stand that is required of me."

The frail, black-robed man came down the little circular staircase from his pulpit. He stood behind the communion tables and lifted his hands to bless the bread and wine. The people began to come forward, to take their places at the tables. Calvin watched them with piercing eyes, waiting for the swaggering figure of Berthelier to move toward him. It never came.

Calvin did not know the reason for Berthelier's absence. He only knew that he had publicly opposed a decision of the Little Council and that he could expect their judgment upon him. Home to the house on Canon Street he went and prepared for the afternoon sermon. It would be his farewell sermon, his last words in Saint Pierre before the councils would order him to leave again. The Libertines had won their victory—what else could he believe? They would free Servetus and let him spread his wicked doctrines in the city from which Calvin would be exiled. This, then, was the end. And God alone knew why.

The afternoon Scripture was Paul's message of farewell to the elders at Ephesus. It might almost have been written for Calvin's farewell to Geneva. ". . . You know . . . after what manner I have been with you at all seasons, serving the Lord . . . with many tears. . . ." The voice from the pulpit trembled. The thin hands gripped the carved railing. ". . . And now . . . I know that ye . . . shall see my face no more. . . . Take heed therefore unto yourselves, and to all the flock . . . for I know this, that after my departing shall grievous wolves enter in among you. . . . And now, brethren, I commend you to God, and to the word of His grace. . . ."

But the herald with the silver-topped stick did not come to the house on Canon Street to order Calvin into exile again.

Surprised at his reprieve, Calvin went on with the press of duties, and with the trial of Servetus.

Servetus was usually in good spirits. The lice and the stench of the prison bothered him terribly, but the news from the jailer, a Libertine, was good. Servetus expected that the enemies of Calvin would win and that he would be freed. He was even so bold as to write the Little Council, "Therefore, my lords, I demand that my false accuser be punished, . . . that his property be awarded to me in recompense for mine, . . . and that he be kept a prisoner as I am until the trial be decided by his death or mine or some other punishment." It is interesting that even Servetus himself expected that the verdict of the trial might well be death, but he did not expect that he would be the one to die.

Against Calvin's advice, the Little Council decided to send for opinions from the churches and city councils of four Swiss cities. The council had asked such advice before and received mild replies. Backed by such mild replies again, the Little Council could free Servetus.

But this time the replies from Zurich, Bern, Basel, and Schaffhausen were a surprise—in fact, a shock to the Libertines. There was nothing mild about them. One council and church after another denounced

Servetus and said that his blasphemies must be stopped before he further injured the church of Christ. In our city, said Bern, the penalty would be death by fire.

The last of the replies came to Geneva on October 18. Ami Perrin did some quick maneuvering. First he claimed to be ill to stall off a decision. Then he asked to have the matter transferred to the Council of Two Hundred, where the Libertines had more strength. But the Little Council was jealous of its powers and would not turn over the case. It was ready to sentence Servetus. For the crime of denying the Trinity and the crime of opposing the baptism of infants and because "you have obstinately tried to infect the world with your stinking heretical poison, . . . we now in writing give final sentence and condemn you, Michael Servetus, to be bound and taken to Champel and there attached to a stake and burned with your book to ashes."

This was the verdict of the Little Council. It was a unanimous verdict because even the Libertines realized they could not ignore the opinions from four influential cities. Calvin heard of the sentence and at once begged the Little Council to substitute the sword for the stake, because beheading was more merciful than burning. But the Little Council quickly refused this request, too.

Servetus heard the verdict in his dirty prison cell and was so stunned by it that he "moaned like a madman" for hours. Then he became quiet, almost humble, though he remained firm in his own beliefs. Calvin went to see him. Servetus asked his forgiveness. Calvin replied, pleading with him as he had done before, "Believe me, never did I have the intention to

197

prosecute you because of some offense against me. Do you remember how, in danger of death, I waited to meet you in Paris nineteen years ago in order to win you to our Lord? And afterwards when you were a fugitive, was I not concerned to show you the right way in letters until you began to hate me because you were offended by my firmness? . . . But . . . ask forgiveness of the everlasting God whom you have blasphemed. . . . Be reconciled to the Son of God . . . to the Saviour."

Farel had come to Geneva. He also pleaded with Servetus. But Servetus, though he went to the stake in fear and not with the joy of many Protestant martyrs, held to his convictions. Farel walked with him out of the city and up the hill to the place of his death. Earlier Farel had chided Calvin for wanting the sword instead of the fire. Maybe now Farel could bear to see Servetus' last moments.

With his book tied to his arm, his body chained to the stake, Servetus died in the flames on the hill called Champel. He was forty-two years old. It was October 27, 1553.

So died the man whose name would be forever linked with that of Calvin. It had been linked because of the burning; yet Calvin was the only person to plead against the use of the stake. The decision to kill Servetus was not Calvin's nor was it caused by his strong influence. It was the verdict of the Little Council of Geneva, upon advice from sister cities. These facts have often been forgotten.

But Calvin did have a share in the death of Servetus. He had asked the councils to arrest the Spaniard. He had brought charges against him. He had carried on the debate before the Little Council to prove that this man's heresy was threatening the church of Christ. And though Calvin had no part in the actual verdict to kill Servetus, he did approve of it, though he opposed death by fire. "The heretic . . . self-condemned," Calvin called him. He even wrote a small book defending the death sentence.

Other Protestant leaders also approved of that death sentence. The mild Melanchthon, always leaning toward peace and compromise, wrote Calvin, "The church of Christ will be grateful to you. . . . Your government has proceeded in the death of this blasphemer according to all laws." This was an age of stakes, an age when men still believed it was their duty to judge other men's beliefs about God.

Today there is a stone on the spot where Servetus died. It was put there long afterward by followers of Calvin. On the stone is this inscription in French: "As reverent and grateful sons of Calvin, our great Reformer, repudiating his mistake, which was the mistake of his age, and according to the true principles of the Reformation and the Gospel, holding fast to freedom of conscience, we erect this monument of reconciliation on this 27th of October, 1903."

Looking back from this twentieth century, it is sad to see that Calvin in his treatment of Servetus acted like other men of his own day. It is sad because in his writings and in much that he did Calvin was far ahead of his time, pointing the way to tolerance and freedom, to separation of church and state, to every man's right to believe in God as his conscience dictates.

The miracle is that God used a sinful servant like John Calvin as mightily as He did to build His church and influence His world.

35

The bitter struggle in Geneva was almost over. There was one more big fracas, but it was like the convulsion of a dying animal. The Libertines were on their way out. They had lost the battle of Servetus as well as the battle of Berthelier and the Lord's Supper. Above all, they had completely lost the support of the people. The elections of February 1555 put into office four syndics who favored Calvin's program for the church and city. Geneva, the Sodom to which Calvin had come, was being transformed into a city of God.

The Libertines made a last try. They seized on the issue of the French refugees who were making Geneva their new home. Through the years, thousands had arrived and were becoming upright citizens of the city.

Down with the foreigners who will betray us to France, cried the Libertines. Geneva belongs to Genevans. Unable to stir up decent people, the Libertines rounded up the riffraff—loafers, transients, peddlers, rowdies, fishermen, and tavern keepers. Berthelier and Ami Perrin wined and dined their recruits at dinner parties before giving them their orders. The plan was that on a certain night, after the nine o'clock sentry had made his rounds, the recruits were to kill any Frenchmen they could find, pretending that the Frenchmen had attacked them first.

But when the night of the attack came, the motley crowd became confused. After all, they had been eating and drinking since noon of that day, and everything looked a little blurred by evening. Turned loose to do their dirty work, they succeeded only in making a lot of noise and in staggering stupidly through the streets. Even those who were sober enough to have their swords ready found no victims. For, reported Calvin, "the Lord Himself . . . kept watch over these refugees and put them into a sound sleep. . . . Not one of them left his house."

The councils had had enough. The Libertines were brought to trial. Berthelier, Vandel, and Perrin—with his impossible Francesca—fled to Bern and escaped their death sentences. But seven others paid with their lives.

After many stormy years, peace had come to Geneva. While peoples and countries around it were rocked with wars and troubles, the city on the lake moved steadily to its place as Reformation city of the world. Because of the man in the house on Canon Street, it was the headquarters of the Protestant faith for all the world of its day.

This was the city of which John Knox, the great reformer of Scotland, said, "Here exists the most perfect school of Christ which has been since the days of the apostles on earth." John Knox lived for three years in Geneva. He became a citizen of the city. He preached to the English refugees in the little auditorium next to Saint Pierre, the auditorium where Calvin lectured on weekdays. In 1559 Knox returned to Scotland and made his homeland the cradle of the

Presbyterian church, a church which followed the doctrine and church government set forth by Calvin.

Farel was another person who had something to say about Geneva. He visited it often. "Better to be the last in Geneva than the first somewhere else," said the red-bearded reformer, remembering the days when this had not been so.

The laws were strict in the Reformation city. From all-out wickedness to all-out godliness—nothing less would do. And there were laws to protect the people as well as to punish them. Calvin influenced the councils to pass health and safety laws, some of the first such laws in Europe.

Dump no garbage or human refuse in the streets. Build no fires in rooms without chimneys. Put railings on balconies so that children cannot fall from them. Nurses, do not take the babies in your care to bed with you. Landlords, rent no rooms without police permission. Sentries, attend to your night watches faithfully. Merchants, do honest business and do not overcharge for your merchandise. Men of Geneva, no paid soldiers will be recruited in our city to serve any other king or country.

These were some of the new laws. And when election time rolled round, the preacher in Saint Pierre was sure to preach a sermon on the duty of citizens to elect godly men, and the duty of elected men to rule by God and for Him.

The preacher of Saint Pierre was also lawyer, diplomat, and specialist in all things. More and more the councils turned to him for his expert advice. He kept himself informed on everything. And why not? Wasn't everything in the world to be studied and used for God's glory? So when the first dentist came to town, he was sent to Calvin. Calvin used his own mouth to test the skill of the man before recommending him for a license. When someone painted a picture to commemorate a treaty with Bern, Calvin was asked to play the art critic and approve it. A man invented a cheaper way to heat homes—what did Calvin think of this, asked the councils?

When the important treaty with Bern had to be renewed, though Bern had a personal dislike for Calvin, he was the man appointed by Geneva to work out the new terms. It was a ticklish situation because Bern had always tried to keep its hand in Geneva's affairs. Yet now, for the first time, a treaty was signed and sealed in which the Bern bear recognized the city on the lake as fully its equal.

How was it possible that the man who did all these things was not even a citizen of his city? He could have been. But he had never asked to be made a citizen lest someone think he was making a bid for power. Thousands of refugees had been given citizenship when they asked for it. Yet Calvin, known all over Europe as "the man of Geneva," was still a foreigner in the city he made famous.

In the final years of Calvin's life, his books continued to come from the printing presses. He left the world ninety-six of them. The commentaries, which were his lectures taken down by secretaries and edited by Calvin himself, covered all the books of the Bible except nine in the Old Testament and the New Testament Book of Revelation. His pen was never still, and he kept several secretaries busy, too. Letters, letters, letters—thirty-five folio volumes of them have been saved, and these are not all. Because of the faithful secretaries, who wrote as Calvin preached, more than two thousand sermons were also saved.

The church of Geneva now knew peace and progress. The number of ministers reached eighteen. The consistory had real power over matters of the church, also over excommunication. And the music of the church—what a thrill it was to hear the psalm-singing people of Geneva. For seventeen years they had a famous singing teacher, Louis Bourgeois, the man who wrote the music for "Praise God from Whom All Blessings Flow." Bourgeois taught both the children and the adults to sing the psalms. He was the first to post psalm numbers on a bulletin board in church. In 1562 the *Genevan Psalter* was published, with many melodies written by Bourgeois. The words were those of Clement Marot and Theodore Beza, but the guiding hand was that of Calvin. In the Geneva Psalter of 1562 he had given the world another treasure.

Yet the greatest glory of the final years was the Geneva Academy, the first Protestant university in the world. For many years it had been Calvin's dream. It was his great conviction that God wants His servants to be educated, well-trained, superior people— the ministers especially, but also the government officials, the doctors, the lawyers, and every other kind of person.

Could Geneva have a university to train such servants for God? The city on the lake had no prince or cardinal to give his name and fortune to a school. It had grown to twenty thousand people, but one-third of them were refugees who had arrived penni-less. To the astonishment of the rest of Europe, Geneva proceeded to build a university. Each of her citizens sacrificed to have a part in it. A poor baker's wife could give only five coins, but a well-to-do printer made up for her and gave the new school a big part of his fortune. And so it went, all through the city. Lawyers drawing up wills for the dying asked them to remember the university in their bequests.

Timber by timber, the school was built on a small hill "swept by winds from the east and south," not far from Saint Pierre. Calvin often dragged himself over to watch the building go up. He had been in bed for months with a kind of malaria caught from mosquitoes in the swampy moats around the city. He never really recovered from the marsh fever, and it plagued him along with all his other ailments. Yet he had to see the progress of the building—the dream coming true.

Perhaps it was his idea that in the arched roof of the porch, which was supported by granite pillars, there should be three texts in three languages. "The fear of the Lord is the beginning of wisdom," said the text in Hebrew, the language of the Old Testament. "Christ has become to us the wisdom of God," said the one in Greek, the tongue of the New Testament. And in Latin, the language of scholars, the text was, "The wisdom which comes from above is pure, peaceful, and full of mercy."

You can go to Geneva today and find much of the building still standing, enlarged by wings on either side, and used as a high school. But the center part is largely as Calvin knew it and walked in it and lectured to the boys who sat before him. Under the front porch is an original, dark classroom, which today's boys jokingly call "the dungeon," because they take their final examinations there.

What was a university without a faculty? And what was a faculty if it was not the best? Calvin wrote to Paris and to other places to invite leading Protestant scholars to teach in the new school. Just at this time, the well-known faculty at Lausanne was having a long dispute with Bern, which controlled that area. Beza, Viret, and a few of their colleagues decided to leave the university at Lausanne rather than compromise their convictions. They were appointed, along with others, to the new university in Geneva. Beza was made the rector. Calvin served as one of the professors. In fact, the faculty was there before the building was finished.

Trumpets and the great Clemence bell called the people to Saint Pierre on June 5, 1559. This was the inauguration service of Geneva Academy. The Secretary of the Little Council read the laws of the school, written by Calvin. Professors were installed. Students pledged themselves to the Reformed confession of faith. Beza, the forty-year-old rector, gave a fine address in Latin. And Calvin, the man whose dream was coming true, spoke in French. He spoke briefly, "as was his habit," and closed the meeting with prayer. It must have been a wonderful day for him.

To the continued astonishment of the rest of Europe, the school was a success from the beginning. Imagine it—soon nine hundred boys were enrolled! They came from all over Europe, many of them from France. After the undergraduate years, some stayed to study theology, medicine, and law.

The students came out of the Academy as well-trained scholars. "The boys of Geneva's academy can speak like doctors of the Sorbonne"—this was their reputation. But they were more than scholars. They were Christian scholars, graduates of the first Protestant university in the world. In the years that followed, many well-known men counted themselves alumni of the Geneva Academy. Among them was Caspar Olevianus, co-author of the Heidelberg Catechism.

What a headquarters for the Reformation faith Geneva had become! It had a world-famous leader, a well-governed church true to the Word, a city committed to the Reformation in life as well as in word, and now, to train Christian scholars, the first Protestant university.

From this headquarters preachers and missionaries went out to all Europe. They stood at Calvin's door, begging to be sent. Many of them were Frenchmen, pleading to be sent to their native land. "They besiege my door," Calvin wrote a friend. "They fight with each other for the posts. . . . Sometimes I try to keep them back. . . . I remind them that in more than twenty towns missionaries have been killed by the people. But nothing can stop them." Not even the French king, who sent an official warning to Geneva, complaining of all the preachers coming from the Protestant headquarters.

1559 was a great year.

In May the underground Reformed church of France held its first national synod in Paris. While its people suffered tortures and death for their faith, the church was organized and adopted the form of church government that Calvin had set forth. Calvin was at that synod in spirit and through letters. This was the church of his homeland. He loved it. He guided it.

From a headquarters far distant, he was its devoted leader.

In June the Geneva Academy was formally opened. It became a model for many other Protestant universities of later years.

In July, Calvin had his fiftieth birthday. Despite his illnesses, he could look around him and thank God for what had been accomplished in Geneva. He was grateful, too, for being spared from death by the marsh fever the year before. During those months of grave illness he had been struggling to finish a final edition of the *Institutes*. It was much bigger than the earlier ones. On some of the worst days of his illness, he did not expect to live long enough to complete his work.

The Lord had spared him. Now, in August of 1559, the final edition came from the presses—eighty chapters in four great volumes. The Lord had been good. He had not deserved it. Nor did he know that he had been spared to finish the Protestant masterpiece which would speak to the world for centuries.

In November of 1559, one of the councilmen suggested that a minister should come to every council meeting, to read from the Bible and to pray for God's blessing on the affairs of the city. This became the honored custom in all three councils of Geneva. The Word of God, preached from the pulpit, taught in the academy, had now been given its place also in the government of the city.

And in December, on Christmas Day, there was one more reason for happiness. The men of the Little Council, contrary to all custom, invited Calvin to become a citizen of Geneva. He was so moved that he could hardly find words to thank them.

But the year had a sober ending. On the same Christmas Day that he was made a citizen, Calvin had a violent coughing spell. The coughing brought a stream of blood from his mouth. "This is the bursting of an artery," said Calvin's doctor, not recognizing sure signs of advanced tuberculosis.

The man on Canon Street had four and a half years left to live.

36

The black-robed man walking over the cobblestones looked more dead than alive, except for his eyes which blazed as brilliantly as always. The body was half-dead, crippled and protesting and refusing to play its part. But the unconquerable spirit demanded that the body make its daily rounds. And the mind behind the piercing eyes had lost none of its keenness.

Calvin stood in the pulpit of Saint Pierre. He lectured in the little auditorium across from the church. He pulled himself up the steps to the classrooms in the academy. And then he went home to bed. Secretaries gathered around the bed. They wrote down the words that came between hard rasping breaths. Letters went out, especially to France where civil war threatened to break out between the Protestants and Catholics. A new commentary was dedicated. Another writing was completed on some controversial doctrine. Missionaries were sent out. Churches received advice. Books came from the printers' presses. And so the work went on.

"By companies, by squadrons, and in single attacks the horde of enemies has invaded me," wrote Calvin to some doctors of Montpellier who had been consulted on his illnesses. "It is twenty years since I have been without a headache." Arthritis and gout crippled the joints of his legs and arms. Kidney stones too large to be passed caused an agony of knifing pain. His chest felt as if a weight were lying on it, and each breath was an effort. But there was no complaint from the man attacked by this army of illnesses. With a wry bit of humor he wrote Beza, who was out of the city on a trip, "You write me long after midnight, while I go to bed at seven, as is my habit. But that is what gouty old men come to."

One day in 1562 Calvin still found strength to leave the city. For the second time, the tragedy of adultery had struck the circle of his own family. He could not bear to stay in the house on Canon Street, so ashamed and stricken he was. The first time, in 1557, it had been Antoine's wife, Ann, caught in adultery with Calvin's hunchbacked servant Pierre. Pierre had been stealing from his master for two years—this, too, had been discovered. Ann had been banished from the city. Antoine had received a divorce and later remarried. The house on Canon Street was never quite the same again.

And now, in 1562, it was Judith, the daughter of Idelette, the girl whom everyone respected as virtuous and godly. Six years earlier she had married happily—and now she stood before the consistory, confessing the adultery of which she was accused. Distressed and ashamed, Calvin managed to get to the country place of Antoine to hide himself a few days. Then back to Canon Street. Back to work. When friends begged him to rest, to stop, he shook his head and answered, "What? Would you want the Lord to find me idle when He comes?"

On Sunday, February 6, 1564, Calvin stood for the last time in the familiar pulpit of Saint Pierre. He was preaching about the harmony of the gospels when the cough seized him. This time he could not stop it. The blood was hot in his mouth. Slowly, reluctantly, he came down the circular staircase, his sermon unfinished. In anxious silence the congregation watched.

The Wednesday before, Calvin had preached his last weekday sermon on the Books of Kings. And in the academy, on the same day in the afternoon, he had given his last lecture on Ezekiel.

It was time for farewells.

First to the town hall, where he had gone so often, in defeat and victory, invited and uninvited. He went—he was carried there near the end of March. He wanted to present to the Little Council a new rector for the academy. Beza would be relieved of the rector's work in order to become Calvin's successor.

There were no longer any stairs to climb to the third floor council chamber. To make it easier for Calvin, the councils earlier had replaced the steps with a ramp, a paved ramp of pebbles that went up alongside the courtyard. Calvin climbed it for the last time, supported by a friend on either side. It was all so familiar. Through a large waiting room to the first door of the Little Council chamber. Here sat the herald on his wooden lion, with his silver-topped staff of authority. Through the first door into the short, narrow corridor. On one side of this passageway a steep spiral staircase went down into one of the prisons so that prisoners could be brought up for trial. Then a second door, and beyond it the Little Council room. Four windows in it, carved desks, and in a corner, a five-sided green tile stove to heat the room.

The new rector was introduced and installed. Then Calvin, holding his cap in his hand, spoke briefly to the Little Council. He thanked the men for their great kindness to him during his illness. Two days before he had felt better, he said, but now it seemed "that nature can endure no more." The clerk dipped his quill into the inkhorn and wrote that Calvin spoke "with great difficulty in breathing and with a marvellous gentleness which all but brought tears to the eyes of the councilmen. And this was the last time he went to the council chamber."

Over the door through which he left the town hall was the motto on Geneva's coat of arms: *Post Tenebras Lux.* "After Darkness Light." More than any other man, Calvin had made that motto come true in the city on the lake.

First to the town hall. Next to Saint Pierre.

It was Easter Sunday, April 2. The men who carried Calvin in his chair from Canon Street placed him near the pulpit from which he had preached hundreds of sermons. Now Beza preached. The Lord's Supper was celebrated. Calvin received the bread and wine from Beza's hand. Did he remember, sitting there for the last time, the Easter before his first exile when he had refused to celebrate the Supper because of the wickedness of the people?

The congregation stood to sing the final song. Their stirring unison filled the vaulted roof. Calvin sang, too, with joy on his face. "Now lettest thou thy servant depart in peace, according to thy word"—this was the final hymn.

From his bed a final letter in French went to the Duchess of Ferrara in France, reassuring her, urging her to win a niece for the Reformed faith. A final letter in Latin went to Bullinger, the reformer in Zurich, with the latest news of France and Germany. Even on his deathbed Calvin kept a keen eye on the world. In neither letter was there mention of his approaching death. The death was not important—only that the progress of the church continue uninterrupted.

A notary came to make Calvin's will. Not that there was much to will away. The greatest legacy Calvin had received could not be counted in money. He spoke of it first. "In the first place, I give thanks to God," he said while the notary wrote. "He drew me out of the abyss . . . to the light of His gospel . . . He has so far extended His mercy toward me as to use me and my work to . . . announce the truth of His gospel . . . He will show Himself the Father of so miserable a sinner."

"The little earthly goods" were easily distributed. To "my well-beloved brother Antoine" a silver cup which Calvin had received from a friend. This as a token of love, so that money could be left to Antoine's children. To the academy ten crowns, and ten to the fund for needy foreigners. To niece Jane, daughter of stepsister Marie, ten crowns. To the sons of Antoine forty crowns each, to the daughters thirty each—

except for nephew David, who was to receive only twenty-five crowns "because he has been thoughtless and unsettled." And if somehow there is more to the estate than these few hundred crowns, the rest is also to be divided among the nieces and nephews, "not excluding David, if God shall have given him grace to be more moderate and sober." Six ministers and one professor signed as witnesses after the notary had read the will in a loud voice for all of them to hear.

There was still a little time for final messages to those who would carry on the work of the church and the city.

On April 30 the Little Council, robed and in procession, arrived at Canon Street and gathered around Calvin's bed. Again Calvin thanked the men for all their kindnesses. He asked their forgiveness for his anger and for his other sins during the years he had served them. He counselled and warned and encouraged. "Remember always," he said, "that it is God alone who gives strength to states and cities." Earnestly he prayed for the councils and for the city. To each man he gave his right hand in farewell. The men went out of the bedroom, weeping, "as if taking their last leave of a father."

The next day the ministers came. Somehow Calvin found strength to speak to them, too, and for a long time. He reminisced. He could still feel the dogs at his heels, snapping at his gown and legs, set on him by disgruntled citizens. He could still hear the sound of forty or fifty musket shots fired under his window before the trip into exile. And the scene in the town hall courtyard when the Two Hundred got into a fight—that also Calvin relived. "You will have troubles, too, when God shall have called me away," he warned the pastors. "But take courage . . . for God will use this church and will maintain it, and promises you that He will protect it."

"My sins have always displeased me. . . . I pray you, forgive me the evil, and if there was any good, . . . make it an example." As to my doctrine, "I have taught faithfully, and God has given me grace to write . . . as faithfully as it was in my power." In this doctrine I have lived and wish to die. Persevere, all of you, in it. "Love one another, support one another. Let there be no envy."

Again the handshake with them all. Again the line of weeping men, stepping out into Canon Street.

There was one more message. To whom but to Farel, the friend of many years. Farel had offered to come. Calvin thought of his friend's old age and wished to spare him the trip from Neuchâtel. "Farewell, best and dearest brother," he wrote, his brother Antoine putting the words on paper. "And since God wills that you should remain the survivor, remember our friendship, which has been useful to the church of God, and whose fruits await us in heaven. Do not weary yourself to come to me. I am already breathing with difficulty, and expect every hour that my breath will fail me altogether. It is enough that I live and die unto Christ, who is the reward for those who are His, in life and death. I commend you, and the brothers who are with you, to God. Devotedly yours, John Calvin."

But Farel came anyway, and sat at the bedside of the man he had ordered to stay in Geneva twenty-eight years before. The two friends talked. And then the seventy-five-year-old Farel went home, walking as he had come, to live one more year before he joined his friend.

Calvin lingered until May 27. He prayed continually, aloud or silently, with his lips moving. In the throes of pain he often cried, "How long, O Lord?" Or, "Lord, Thou dost crush me, but it suffices that it is Thy hand."

He died peacefully, as one falls asleep. It was a Saturday evening—the end of a day, the end of a week, the end of a life. A great servant had gone to his Master.

Hearing the news, the people of Geneva gathered silently outside the house on Canon Street. The Little Council met in special session. The clerk, trying to record the feelings of the councilmen, wrote with his quill, "God marked him with a character of such majesty and loftiness—." In the minutes of the consistory, opposite the name of Calvin, which was marked with a cross, there were these words, "Gone to God, May 27 of this present year, between eight and nine o'clock in the evening."

On Sunday afternoon at two the procession went to the city churchyard, the Plain-Palais cemetery just outside the city. Professors, ministers, councilmen, and citizens were in the great crowd that followed the pine coffin. Only the sound of many feet broke the Sunday stillness.

Calvin had asked in his will that "my body . . . be interred in the usual manner, to wait for the day of the blessed resurrection." So there were no words at the grave. No stone was placed to mark the spot. Soon no one knew where Calvin's body lay. The grave remains unknown today.

But something greater, something living has remained. Through the centuries the ideas and writings of the man of Geneva have remained powerfully alive. Drawn from the living Word, they have reached out into all the Christian world. Through them the preacher of Saint Pierre has been teaching and shaping the church of Christ. He has been speaking in the lives of men and of nations.

This was John Calvin, mighty servant of Jesus Christ. This was the humble man who lived by a motto. *Soli Deo Gloria*, said the man of Canon Street. To God alone the glory.

Index

220